THE STORY OF GOWER

THE STORY OF GOWER

WENDY HUGHES

Gwasg Carreg Gwalch

Dedication

For my husband Con with thanks for encouraging and supporting me through many a stormy situation and bringing me safely to drier and happier islands.

Contents

Author's Note

This book could not have been written without reference to the many authors who have researched Wales and the peninsula before me. A selected list appears at the end of this book.

I would like to express my thanks to the following people, whose assistance and help made the task of writing this book easier.

Con Hughes, who walked the length and breadth of Gower to take the cover photographs and a majority of the black and white photographs.

The Welsh Folk Museum and The National Museum of Wales for permission to use some of their photographs.

Mr Robert L. T. Lucas for his help with the Lucas family and providing the answers to several queries.

Dilys Gater and all my writing friends, who had faith in my ability to write a book.

Myrddin ap Dafydd, my publisher, who gave me the opportunity to write about such an interesting area.

Introduction

The Gower Peninsula has such a unique combination of natural beauty, history, and customs, that at first sight it is impossible for the visitor to appreciate its full potential.

In an area that is no more than sixteen miles long by seven miles wide, and narrowing to just four miles, the scenes change like a kaleidoscope, leaving the observer spellbound in awed wonder. The scenery tranforms from neatly bordered fields to wild rugged moorlands, from sheltered bays that once hid the activities of smugglers, to bleak isolated cliff tops, scene of the wreckers and their wicked activities. The impressive churches cast their solemn eyes down on the tiny cottages, that could tell countless tales of mystery and suspense. Nature too is not forgotten with its unique abundance of rare flowers, bird sanctuaries and the fishing industries.

Every period of history is represented, from the early cave dwellers of the Cro-Magnon period to the fighting Norse warriors, from the flamboyant Tudors to the turbulent times of smugglers and wreckers. But it was the horse-bus proprietors and road builders of the 1920s who opened up a new frontier to the outside world for the people of Gower.

With such beauty it is little wonder that Gower was one of the first places to be designated 'An Area of Outstanding Natural Beauty' under the Act of 1949.

Gower, or Gŵyr in Welsh, has always belonged to a larger area. Between the 7th and 9th centuries 'Guhir' was part of the Seisyllwg of ancient Deuheubarth, which by the 10th century was under the rule of that famous Lawmaker, Hywel Dda, or Howell the Good. In medieval times it was one of the three Commotes of the cantref of Ystrad Tywi, which was part of the cantref of Morgannwg. Legend also informs that Gower was at one time given to Uhen Rheged, one of King Arthur's Knights. In 1536, during the reign of Henry VIII, it finally became part of Glamorgan.

In such a short book it is impossible to tell the whole story of Gower. I have tried through its richly woven tapestry of legends, notorious characters and history to tell you enough to make you want to learn more about this corner of Wales.

There's a saying in Wales, 'See Gower in an Hour,' but I challenge anyone to try it. Even a fortnight may seem too short, but come equipped with wellingtons. The beauty can be guaranteed, but not the weather!

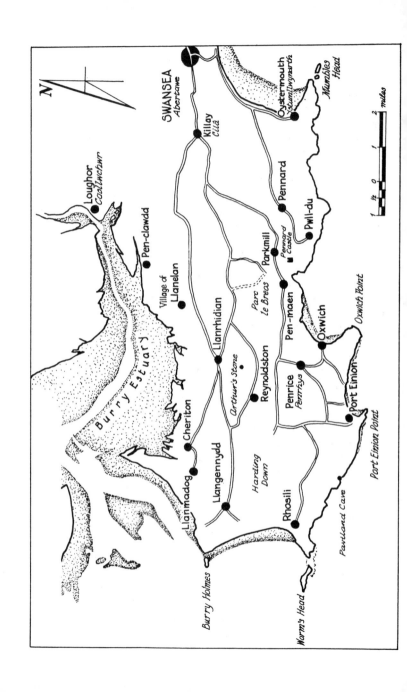

CHAPTER ONE

The Earliest Gowerians

To begin our story of the Gower Peninsula we must go back in time, in fact 20,000 years to the end of the Ice Age. At that time Britain was still attached to Europe, and the climate was vastly different from that we experience today. Long periods of much colder conditions alternated with periods when the climate was much hotter than anything we know today.

These facts can be proved by the strange collection of bones found along the Gower Peninsula. For example, the mammoth and reindeer would have adapted well to the sub-zero temperatures; the rhinoceros, straight tusked elephant, lion and hippopotamus would have basked in the warmer climate, unable to cope with the so-called mild temperatures of present day Britain.

At the end of the last Ice Age, huge cliffs sweeping down towards a wide valley formed an edge to the wind-swept Gower Peninsula. In this valley, where the Bristol Channel now is, would have roamed some of the exotic animals whose remains fascinate us today.

As yet, man had not acquired any of the basic skills of the farmer or the herdsman. He lived off the animals he could hunt and kill, together with any wild berries he could gather. It was really a case of the survival of the fittest, and often the fastest.

These nomadic hunters moved widely over Northern Europe in pursuit of herds of mammoth and reindeer, which provided early man with the food and clothing essential to maintain him through these cold periods. As the ice slowly receded they would have used the caves around the Gower Coast as seasonal shelters.

One of these caves, Paviland, also known as Goat's Cave, made the headlines in 1823, when it was excavated by the Reverend William Buckland, the first Professor of Geology at Oxford University.

Excitement was generated when Buckland discovered part of a headless human skeleton, still wearing a necklace of wolf and reindeer teeth. The bones were stained red, and it is assumed that, during the burial ritual, the body would have been covered in red ochre as part of the ceremony to liven up the pallid corpse. Alongside the skeleton Buckland found the bones of mammoth, rhinoceros, some ivory shaped tools, and a skewer made from the metarcapal bone of a wolf. He assumed that the animal bones had been washed into the caves by the tide, and that the skeleton was that of a priestess from the ancient Romano British time. The skeleton became known as 'The Red Lady of Paviland'.

However, in 1913 Professor Sallas of the Geology Department at Oxford, re-excavated the cave. With more modern techniques he discovered that the 'lady' was in fact a slender young man of the Paleolithic period, the old Stone Age, and the earliest form of man as we know him today. He would have been more heavily built than modern man, but otherwise he had the same anatomical characteristics. He was aged about 25 and may have belonged to a group of hunters, possibly descended from people who lived in a rock shelter in the Dordogne in France. There, in 1868, the skeletons of four adults and an infant were found, along with the first masterpieces in decorative art. We are tempted to call this young man of Paviland our first Gowerian, and, although this isn't strictly true, I'm sure most will excuse the slight exaggeration.

Many slender ivory rings and bone needles have been found around Gower, indicating that our young hunter of Gower was better clothed than modern cartoons and films would have us believe. From these findings and some of the rare engravings on bone that have survived, it appears that he would have been dressed in a close fitting fur suit, similar to that of the nineteenth century Eskimo.

In 1912 there was further excitement in Gower when ten strange horizontal bands of dark red markings were discovered in a cavern in Bacon Hole. Could these series of lines have represented a net or a trap for catching big game? Could similar paintings to those found in Lascaux lurk in the deep recesses of our Gower caves? Welsh archaeologists were unsure, so an expert, Abbe Breuil, was invited from France to examine the scratchings. After careful consideration, he rubbed his chin and said, 'Yes, they could be.' The archaeologists were delighted, and immediately an iron grille was placed around the markings to protect them. As the years passed, so they slowly changed shape, and it was discovered that they were only caused by iron oxide seeping naturally from the rocks. So Gower didn't enter the history books alongside Lascaux after all. Today the iron grille is broken and rusted, a fading relic of what might have been.

Reconstruction scene at Paviland Cave

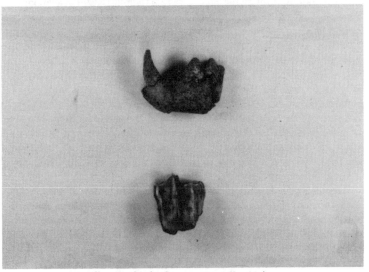

Jaw teeth of a bear or a woolly rhino found in Paviland Cave

But who knows what may be revealed in those numerous dark caverns along the coast? Only time will tell. For now, we have to be content with the most important find at this cave, a bowl of the Paleolithic period, proof that early man did inhabit the cave. An extensive excavation revealed a fine collection of bones, including those of the giant ox, bison, wolf, soft-nosed rhinoceros, and hyena. These are now exhibited on the upper floor of Swansea Museum.

Minchin Hole, the largest of the Gower caves, accessible from the cliff top at Southgate, was excavated in the 1850s by Colonel Wood of Stouthall, and later by Mr J. G. Rutter, former Curator of Archaeology at the Swansea Museum. It is one of the few Gower caves where bones of the lion have been found. Rutter also found evidence of hearths, which proved that the cave had been occupied in the Roman and Dark Age periods, and it was thought that, at one time, it could have been an anchorite cell. At the time Rutter claimed that this was the most important native settlement in the first few centuries of the Christian era yet found in Wales. Because of its large size it could possibly have been used as a safe haven for the people of Pennard during unsettled times.

We learn that the early hunters ventured inland too, for just past the mill at Parkmill, through the valley, we find Cathole Cave. Excavations in 1968 revealed a quantity of flint blades which were found in a thick layer of unweathered limestone fragments. This had broken from around the mouth of the cave as the deep frozen rock began to thaw, indicating that it had once been the home of the Ice Age hunting groups.

Leather's Hole, set high on the east side behind the Great Tor at Pen-maen, revealed the bones of mammoth, wolf, hyena and woolly rhinoceros. Although the cave would have been accessible to man in the last stages of the Ice Age, it would have been impossible for these animals to enter. It is possible that the remains were dragged there by the cave's carnivorous inhabitants, and the bones discarded after they had feasted on the flesh. Today it is possible to enter the cave only by lying flat on the ground and edging forward.

Around 23,000 B.C. a dramatic change occurred in the fortunes of our early ancestors. By now they had learned the art of domesticating animals, sowing seed and growing crops. Some of these first farmers, belonging to what we now call the Neolithic period, had settled in the remotest parts of Gower. They soon learnt the art of building burial chambers out of massive pieces of undressed stone, hence the term, 'megalith' or big stone. Once they had mastered this skill they began to bury those of

The Burial Chamber at Parc le Breos

Entrance to the Burial Chamber

importance in the society with impressive ceremony. One of the best preserved examples of a burial chamber from this period is at Parc le Breos near Parkmill, a little distance from Cathole Cave. There you will find a central wedge-shaped passage with four side chambers in a cairn about 70 ft long. There are two projections at the entrance, in the typical style of the Coltswold-Severn long barrows, and the whole construction would have been covered with a mound of earth or small stones. With the passing of time these covering mounds have worn away, leaving the stones of the burial chamber in isolation to form what we now call a Cromlech, or 'shelter stone.'

The Parc le Breos barrow was first excavated in 1869 by Sir John Lubbock, the man who introduced the word Neolithic — New Stone Age, into the English language. At that time, he thought the cairn was circular, and it was not until 1937, when Professor Glyn Daniel re-excavated that it was discovered to be an elongated barrow. The remains of humans were discovered along with fragments of pottery and a few animal bones. Archaeologists now believe that before the bodies were buried, they were exposed to the elements for the flesh to decompose. It is quite possible that these tombs were used over many years by several generations. Skeletons would have been ritually dismembered and moved around, so that the burial of other individuals could be accommodated.

A fascinating wonder of Gower's Neolithic period can be found on Cefn Bryn. It is 'King Arthur's Stone' — a chambered tomb dating to approximately 2500 B.C. and of uncertain origin. It is capped with a boulder that weighs some 24 tons, encircled by a number of smaller stones. A stone of this size suggests that it was the burial ground of an impressive personage, although curiously, the space beneath is not really large enough for an important figure and all his belongings. No bones have been found here, and some believe that it is the Maen (stone) Cetti, one of the wonders of Ancient Britain. Whatever its purpose it is surrounded by legends.

One states that during the 6th century, St David, fearing a return to Druidism, worshipping of the pagan gods, struck the stone with his staff and split it, proving that it was an altar of the false gods. The stone takes its name from the legend of King Arthur. It is reputed that the King, passing through Carmarthenshire on his way to the battle of Camlon, felt a pebble in his shoe. He stopped, removed the stone, and threw it as far as he could. It fell on Cefn Bryn some seven miles away. It is said that on

King Arthur's Stone

Midsummer's Eve the stone goes down to the shores of the Burry Pill estuary for a drink of water.

There is also a delightful old custom that, at midnight and under a full moon, young girls would test their lovers' fidelity by making a cake from barleymeal and honey. This was wetted with milk before being well kneaded on the stone. Then the girl crawled round the stone three times on all fours, making quite an impressive sight. If her young man appeared it proved that he was faithful and intended to marry her. If he did not show up, then it proved that he wasn't true and never planned to marry her. The girls believed that it was some magical power within the stone that made their young men appear. I suspect that if the young man really wanted to marry his sweetheart he would have arranged for her mother to inform him of the impending test.

Even by the fifteenth century the stone had become a famous 'tourist attraction.' It is recorded that when the Breton troops in Henry VII's army landed at Milford Haven en route to battle at Bosworth Field, they made a slight detour of some eighty miles just to visit this ancient wonder.

At Pen-maen there is another relic of this era, the Megalithic tomb called Pen-y-Crug (the top hillock, or tumulus). It is almost hidden by bracken during the summer months. It dates back to 3000 B.C., an is an excellent example of a communal tomb. It was first excavated in 1893, when human and animal remains were found, together with fragments of pottery. All that survives today are the remnants of an entrance passage with one remaining side chamber which was covered by a massive capstone weighing some 7 tons.

CHAPTER TWO

The Age of Advancement

The next group of people to inhabit our lands were the Beaker folk, who drifted into South Wales about 1900 B.C. These new invaders arrived from the East, mainly from the lands along the Rhine. Unlike the Neolithic folk, who had long skulls, the Beaker people had rounded skulls which linked them to the Alpine Race of Central Europe, and were physically strong and full of energy. They were so called because of the distinctive shape of their pottery, a richly decorated bell-shaped beaker. These beakers were buried along with the dead. It is now thought that they contained a herb-flavoured alcoholic beverage, to sustain the deceased on the journey into the next world.

Unlike the Neolithic people, the Beaker folk buried their dead in round barrows, and a typical barrow would have contained only one corpse — no doubt an important person in the clan or tribe. The uncremated body or skeleton was buried in a scooped out pit, and in a crouched position with head forward, arms and knees bent towards the chin. The grave was then covered by placing earth or stones in a heap around the body, and covering the whole with a dome-shaped mound. Excavators have found evidence that the earth was carried in baskets and tipped over the grave, as frequently a ditch has been found a little distance from the barrow. It is believed that the barrow builders may have traced a circle a short distance from the grave, and formed the mound by heaping inwards the earth dug from the ditch. Other items buried with the body included ornaments, bronze daggers, and clothing. As the period progressed cremation became more frequent, with the edges of these burial mounds being re-used for burials.

The Beaker people built earthwork enclosures and ditches, and there are a number of these throughout Gower, ten perched on Rhosili Downs, twelve on Llanmadog Hill and over seventy on Cefn Bryn. Two were destroyed when Fairwood Airport was built, and most have now been flattened with the passage of time.

As the earlier generation grew older, and their culture passed away, so the newer generation of Beaker folk were responsible for introducing the first known metallurgical technology, and by mixing tin and copper the Bronze Age was born. This new metal was fashioned into axes, swords, sickles and personal ornaments. Few sites from this period have been found in Gower, suggesting that the population was not very large. Those sites discovered were not fortified, although a hoard of swords dating from this period were discovered at Pennard.

Around 1,000 B.C. the western population had increased considerably, and by 500 B.C. the warrior Celts were established. Between them they brought us another new metal, iron, which was easier to work than the copper alloy to make bronze, and more readily available than bronze. This period became known as the Iron Age.

It was a time of warfare between the rival tribes, and the hillforts and earthworks were a conspicuous feature of the landscape. The constructions were of a simply type, a single bank and ditch. The largest Iron Age encampment to be found in Gower is at Cil Ifor Top (Cil being Welsh for retreat), near Llanrhidian. This covers approximately eight acres, and consists of three ramparts and ditches enclosing a steep-sided hill. We know nothing of its history, although the ditches may have been used as communal shelters in times of trouble. It was probably an important encampment because the complex entrances are fitted with timber barricades and pointed stakes.

Its nearest neighbour, the Bulwark on Llanmadog Hill, shows seven separate phases of construction indicating that times were unsettled. Who knows? Maybe these encampments were used by the dwellers to protect themselves from the invading Romans as they advanced into South West Wales. Maybe from their lookout points, our early Gowerians saw the approaching legions pushing their way towards Loughor, only five miles away, and barricaded themselves in their hillfort. As no records exist, alas, we shall never know.

Legend relates that the holders of the Bulwark Fort met the occupants of another nearby encampment called Hardings Down in a fierce encounter. The battle took place on open ground, now known as Tankeylake Moor. It was a brutal battle, and the Bulwark's leader, Tonkin, was killed. The slaughter was so great that the blood of the dead flowed and rose over the great warrior's boots, hence the name Tankey (or Tonkin) Lake.

At Rhosili, near the coastguards' cottages is a rather odd relic, which

Reconstruction of farming settlement 4000 BC

can easily be missed by the unobservant. Backing onto the cliffs is a semi-circle of hollows and bumps known as 'Old Castle'. It is thought to be the site of a defensive village belonging to a tribe of Silures. It would appear to be a rather bleak and remote place for anyone to have settled, although in such times of unrest its remoteness may have been protection.

Above Bluepool, in the dunes, are the remains of a stone walled Iron Age enclosure, while not far away, under the cliffs, is a cave called Llangennydd Culver Hole. It is only accessible at low tide and is seen as a long vertical slit cut into the limestone cliffs. Excavations have revealed the remains of about 30 individuals, and several items of the Iron Age and Roman periods. A number of fragments of pottery have been found which included pieces of up to twelve plain urns of the late Bronze Age. This type of pottery is extremely rare in South Wales, and it is thought to indicate that the cave was used as a resting place for the bones of the dead.

In about 50 A.D. our land was under attack again, this time by the Romans. The Silures put up an excellent fight, but by 78 A.D., the Roman Conqueror, Frontinus Legate, had subdubed the Silures and Gondelic tribes of South East Wales. As we can see, by this time Gower had a mixture of races as inhabitants differed in physical appearance, and possibly language too. Tacitus reporting to his father-in-law Agricola, mentioned the Silures of Glamorgan as people of dark complexions and curly hair, which is still true today. We are still not certain about language, although it is known that at the time of the Romans, Celtic speech had been established in Wales. Roman occupation of Britain lasted until 410 A.D., but there is very little evidence left in the Gower area today.

The Romans saw South Wales as an area of military control, where road and fort constructions were their main priorities. The main military road ran through Neath to Loughor and on to Carmarthen, by-passing Gower. Pottery and Quern stones — which were used as millstones for grinding — and coinage, were found at Loughor, Leucarum in Roman times, in North East Gower, suggesting that a civilised settlement existed some time in the 1st and 3rd centuries. In 1985, because of the increase in traffic, a new road was built through the site of the Roman fort. A 'rescue dig' was hurriedly carried out and revealed some fascinating details about the life of the Roman garrison. For example, around the commandant's house a large amount of oyster shells was excavated suggesting that the Romans must have enjoyed those found in the Oystermouth area. At Swansea Museum there is a Roman altar from Loughor.

Reconstruction of Bronze Age hut

At Oystermouth, known as Ystumllwynarth in Welsh, the remains of a villa have been discovered. In 1860, when the parish church of All Saints was being extended, workmen moved a bank of earth on the south side and accidentally broke up a Roman mosaic paved floor. George Grant Francis, a local amateur archaeologist, collected what he could. Today you can see the red, cream, grey and black cubes set into a slate tablet and displayed in the church. It would seem that an unknown Roman gentleman built himself a villa on our curving seashore, although Swansea itself was never a Roman site. We know that the owners of Chedworth Villa in the Cotswolds are known to have eaten Bristol Channel oysters. Perhaps these were from Oystermouth, and this villa was owned by a gentleman operating an oyster-catching business which was only accessible by sea. We can only surmise.

The length of the Roman occupation in this area is not known. Only pottery and coins from the first and third centuries have been found. The coins excavated at Loughor were minted by Carausius in the third century. A hoard of Roman coins have been discovered in a disused quarry in the valley at Ilston Cwm. At Barland in Bishopston, Roman ironwork, pottery and glass have been recovered, indicating that a Roman settlement stood here during the 2nd century A.D.

At Minchin Hole cave, the Roman period is also represented by a fragment of well-made burnished pottery. This is a piece of Samian ware, mass produced in Central Gaul and traded throughout the Roman Empire. Later, towards the end of the late fourth century, people living or hiding in the same cave left quantities of a coarse 'calcite-gritted' pottery. The curved rim of a storage jar from this period can be seen in Swansea Museum.

When the Romans finally left Britain, it would appear that South Wales took a few steps back in time, and reverted to the Old Iron Age settlements.

Cil Ifor Top near Llanrhidian

CHAPTER THREE

Christianity In Gower

Christianity reached Wales long before the Roman garrisons had left at the beginning of the fifth century. It is believed that the now lost church of Llanelan, once situated in a small wood about a quarter of a mile from the parish of Llanrhidian, was founded in the early part of the 6th century. It was dedicated to Helen of Caernarfon (Elen Luyddog), Welsh wife of Magus Clemens Maximus, Emperor of Britain, Gaul and Spain (383-8), who was killed trying to obtain Roman recognition. This church is mentioned in one of the old Penrice Manuscripts dated 1319. The only remaining evidence of its existence are two ancient stones, although one is inscribed with the date 1687, built into the churchyard at Llanrhidian.

It seems that the Romans actually encouraged the Irish to settle in Gower, because a number of Gower churches were dedicated to Irish Saints.

The church of Bishopston is dedicated to St Teilo, and stands on the site of one of the earliest Christian settlements in Wales. The old name for the village was Llandeilo Ferwallt. This means 'Church of St Teilo near Fairwood'. According to the 'Liber Landavenis' — The Book of Llandaff — the Church dates back to about 480 A.D.

The church at Llangennydd, the largest in Gower, is dedicated to St Cennydd, Gower's own Celtic saint who is reputed to have founded a hermitage nearby in the 6th century. There is an interesting legend relating to the birth of St Cennydd.

The noble prince of Brittany, Dihocus, had a beautiful daughter. Dihocus fell madly in love with his own daughter, and seduced her. Saint Cennydd was the result of their union. King Arthur, who ruled Britain at the time, was holding a court at Loughor on Christmas Day, and Dihocus and his daughter were invited. Although she was heavily pregnant, she went, and gave birth to St Cennydd among the tents. When he was born, the calf of his leg was attached to his thigh. The Prince fearing a scandal, ordered that the child should be cast into the river in a Moses-like wicker

The Church at Bishopston

cradle, hoping that he would drift down the Burry estuary and out to the sea.

A terrific storm blew up and lashed the west coast, but the cradle remained upright and safe. As the wind drove the cradle over the waves, a number of seagulls flew down and held the cradle with their beaks, gently guiding it towards Worm's Head. The seagulls placed the cradle in a hollow in the rocks, and some made a bed of feathers for the boy, while others protected him with their wings. An angel of God placed a little brass bell by the child's head, which has been affectionately named 'THE TITTY BELL', or *cloch tethauc*, from the Latin *cloch* meaning bell and *teth* meaning teat. The bell was shaped like a brazen breast, and it is said that whenever the child was hungry a doe obligingly filled it with milk. The nourishment that flowed from the bell was sweeter than honeycomb, and so pure that no normal bodily functions occurred. The clothes that the child wore grew with him and never decayed. For eighteen years he stayed on Worm's Head taught by an angel, until God instructed him to move to Burry Holmes, about a mile away. On the way, whenever St Cennydd stopped and rested, a spring suddenly appeared — twenty four in all.

Cennydd radiated happiness around him, and his fame spread throughout Gower. He carried his 'Titty Bell' with him, and one touch could enable him to skim the waters to his friend, St David in Pembrokeshire. J. D. Davies in his *History of West Gower*, published in 1879, records that by the mere sound of his bell, St Cennydd once destroyed an army of soldiers. It is also reputed that, through a miracle, St Cennydd's leg was temporarily cured so that he could take part in an important religious convention.

From both archaelogical and documentary evidence it is known that an ecclesiastical settlement existed at Burry Holmes which took the form of a hermitage.

The most interesting feature of Llangennydd church is a stone resting on the centre of the west wall. It is the base of a Celtic cross elaborately carved with an interlacing design. This is reputed to be the coffin lid of the tomb of St Cennydd, and from time immemorial it has been referred to by the local inhabitants as 'Cennydd's Stone'. His skull, a relic which was still in existence in the second half of the 15th century, was used by the people of Llangennydd for swearing formal oaths.

Llangennydd is also the only church in Gower to have a lych-gate. This was presented to the church in 1903, and the carving depicts some of the incidents in the life of St Cennydd, as related by Capgrave in his *Nova*

Llangennydd Church

The lych-gate at Llangennydd Church

Legenda Angliae, printed in Latin and published by Wynkyn de Worde in 1516.

Near the church of Llanmadog, down a lane is the hamlet called Cwm Ivy. It was here, in a field called Parc-yr-Odyn — *the field of the kiln* — in the 1870s, that a farmer ploughed up a curious rectangular shaped bell. It is very roughly made, riveted on one side, and covered with a thin coating of some bright susbstance, thought to be gold. It resembles the ancient sacred bells from Ireland which were carried by all the saints. Could this have been *the* famous 'titty bell' of St Cennydd?

The Church of Llanmadog is dedicated to Madog, a Celtic saint, who is reputed to have founded a church there in the 6th century. On the outside wall, let into the window-sill, is a rare gravestone of the Romano-British period. It was discovered in 1861, in the old Rectory, removed and placed in the Church. The Latin inscription reads: 'DUECTI FILIUS GUAN HIC IACIT' — Duectus son of Guan lies here. The probable date of this stone is 6th century.

There are two other interesting stones in this church. One known as the 'Boundary Stone' was found in the wall of Llanmadog churchyard in 1864. It is probably one of the old boundary stones which were used in ancient times to mark the boundaries of church properties. The stone, which dates from the 7-9th century, is reddish in colour and engraved on both sides. One side depicts a Latin cross with crossleted arms. The other side has a larger cross, again with crossleted arms and a circle at the intersection.

The second stone is a Celtic pillar cross, found in the churchyard, and is now considered to be the old churchyard cross. This church is one of the few Gower churches where medieval wall paintings were uncovered when the church was restored.

The church at Llanrhidian is dedicated to St Illtyd, although some say that it was originally dedicated to a Celtic Saint, St Rhidian, who founded the church in the 6th Century. Inside the porch sits one of the many curiosities of Gower. It is a fragment of a pre-Norman sculptured stone, known locally as the Leper's Stone, and is coffin shaped. It is believed to date from the 9th century, and was identified by Professor Nash-Williams as similar to stones found in the north of England, where they are called 'Hog Backs'. On it the representations of animal figures and human faces are most striking. It was found buried in front of the west tower doorway in 1865 and moved to its present position in 1910. The stone is the only one found in Wales. How a stone associated with the north of England came to rest in Gower is baffling, and its history remains a complete mystery.

Another unusual relic, and the earliest Christian monument to be found in Gower, stands in Reynoldston Church. It is a pillar cross, which was found set into an old mill-stone on top of a mound in a field in Stouthall Park. It was given to the church in 1977 and is made of grey sandstone, roughly rectangular in shape and gently tapered at the top and bottom. One side bears a simple cross, and on the other a cross is cut in relief with a recessed circle. Between the intersection of the arms are two small crosses, under which a pattern of interlaced work can be traced. Below this can be seen a symbol resembling two hooks placed back to back. Unfortunately the design is incomplete because a piece of the stone is missing.

The church at Oxwich, however, is definitely dedicated to St Illtyd, and the foundations date back to the 6th century. It is said that the simple rough font was placed in the church by St Illtyd himself, who is reputed to have lived in holy seclusion at Oystermouth. The church differs from the rest of those in Gower, in that it is entered from the west through a doorway in the tower, the lowest part forming the porch.

One of the most interesting tombstones to be found in Gower must be the family stone discovered at Pen-maen church in 1854-55, during restoration work. The tombstone bears the date 1623, but traces the family tree back to Iestyn ap Gwrgan, who was Lord of Glamorgan in the 11th century. The inscription reads:

> 'Here resteth the body of David sonne of David the sonne of Richard the sonne of Nicholas the sonne of Rys the sonne of Leison the sonne of Rys the sonne of Morgan Ychan the sonne of Morgan the sonne of Craddocke the sonne of Iustin ap Gwrgan sometime Lord of Glamorgan interred the 21 day of August in the year of our blessed redemption 1623. In this bit of earth likewise reposeth the body of Jane his wife deceased the 23 of Febr 1631 whome God consorts in sacred rites and love death cannot seperate marrow from the dove.'

Around the edge of the stone reads:

> Buried heere alsoe Lewis Davids son of David . . . (stone broken here) . . . Iane within named the 4 of November 1647 aged 68 together with Margaret Benet his wife daughter of John Benet of Penrice.'

We can trace the history back to pre-Norman Morgannwg. Iestyn ap Gwrgan was the last Welsh ruler of Morgannwg, and his father Gwrgan, was descended from the line of Welsh kings. When the Norman, Robert Fitzhamon, conquered Morgannwg, Iestyn ap Gwrgan was the ruler. Iestyn then married a daughter of the ruling Prince of Powys, and his descendants must have married into a Norman family, because they were granted lands throughout Morgannwg, including places like Baglan, Miscin, and Kilvey which then came under Gower. They took the surname of Avene.

In 1221, Ilston church in Parmill was presented to the Knights Hospitallers of St John of Jerusalem, by John de Breos, the son of William de Breos. This was mentioned in the Confirmation of Bishop Anselm in 1230, and continued to be held by the Knights Hospitallers until the Dissolution of the Monasteries by Henry VIII in 1540, when it was then passed to the Crown.

In 1649 John Myles was installed by the Parliamentarians as Cromwellian Minister of Ilton, but at the restoration of Charles II in 1660 he was ejected and replaced by William Houghton who was the Minister prior to 1649. John Myles then went on to build the first Baptist church in Wales in Ilston Cwm on the site of the medieval chapel of Trinity Well. Today a simple stone pulpit in the form of an open bible, in memory of John Myles stands on the ruins. A plaque on the front reads:

To
commemorate the foundation
in this valley of the
first Baptist Church in Wales
1649-1660
and to honour the memory of
its founder
John Myles
this ruin is the site of the
pre-reformation Chapel of
Trinity Well
and is claimed by tradition
as a meeting place of the
above Cromwellian Church
the memorial
has been erected with the
permission of
Admiral A. W. Heneage-Vivian
C.B. M.V.O.

Ruins of the first Baptist Church in Wales

John Myles, who was the son of Walter Myles of Newton, Herefordshire, was born in 1621. At the age of fifteen he went of Oxford and matriculated at Brasenose College. He was ejected from the church for refusing, as ordered under the laws of James I, to read the *Book of Sports* from the pulpit. One of the passsages read:

'As for our good people's recreation, our pleasure is that after the end of Divine Service, our good people be not disturbed, letted, or discouraged from any lawful recreation, such as Dancing, either man or woman, Archery for men, leaping, vaulting or any such harmless recreation, or from having Maypoles, Whitson Ales, or Morris dances, and the setting-up of Maypoles and other sports here with used.'

In 1663, when the law against Dissenters was passed. John and his followers emigrated to New England, and founded a Baptist church and the town of Swansea, Massachusetts.

CHAPTER FOUR

Viking and Norman Involvement

Pirate raids began along the coast of Gower in 795 A.D. by Norwegian invaders, who were quickly followed by the Danes and Swedes. There is an entry in the Manual of Dates to the effect that, in 877 A.D., 120 Danish vessels were wrecked in Swansea Bay.

Vikings landed in Rhosili Bay in 986 A.D. and burned the village of Llangennydd, destroying the Priory founded in the 6th century by St Cenydd. It is reputed that while the Danes were busy carrying out their evil deeds, the men of Rhosili crept along the beach under cover of darkness, and burned the Norsemen's boats.

The following year, 987 A.D., Edwin ab Einion, a Welsh prince, together with an army of Danes destroyed lands in West Wales, including Gower. He was probably assisted by the Scandinavian warlord, Sweine Forkbeard, who was Svend Tveskag, King of Denmark from 988-1014 A.D., and gave his name to nearby Swansea. Prince Einion is thought to have built a castle on Port Einion point, although very little is known of its existence. Legend states that Sweine was killed and is buried in Sweine Howe (How meaning mound), a burial chamber on Rhosili Down. This may be true, although the chamber dates back to 2500 B.C. Perhaps it was one of the chambers that was used by a number of generations.

During the 11th century the Normans conquered Rhosili and settled in Gower. The original village and church were tucked to the front of the Down, on a site known today as the Warren. The church dates back to the 6th century, and was dedicated to St Sili which, together with the Welsh word for moorland, Rhos, gives Rhosili its name. During the 10-13th centuries huge sandstorms blew up, lashing the west coast of Gower with rain and wind. Waves crashed inland, and the old village and church were completely engulfed with sand.

The location of the original settlement was not known for sure, but thanks to a severe storm at the end of 1979, streams moved the sand and part of the walls of a house and the church were exposed. A dig was carried out and the remains of the church were revealed and studied prior to back filling for protection. The walls stood almost to their original height, and were of local stone bonded with lime mortar and plastered both inside and out. The site of this settlement and church is now protected by law as an Ancient Monument.

We know that the Normans settled in this village, but there is some evidence that Rhosili was built on the site of a pre-Norman monastic settlement dedicated to St Cynwal. Maybe the church cradled in the sand on the Warren is on the site of an even older Christian building.

The present church and village was built around the 12-13th century, and dedicated to St Mary. Tradition states that the doorway was brought from the old church in the Warren. This was confirmed during the 1980 dig, when the original porch was found to be missing. The doorway is an excellent example of Norman craftmanship, rare in Wales, and unique to Gower. We can also tell that the former building must have had its doorway facing the sun, as there is a scratch sundial on the left post. This would have had a stick inserted in the hole and the time read from the shadow cast on the scratched lines denoting the hours.

By the 11th century, a Norman king was seated on the English throne. Shortly after 1100 A.D., the Normans seized Gower from the Welsh ruler and the ancient Welsh Cantref of Gŵyr became the Norman Lordship of Gower.

The early castles were not of the stone type that remain today, but of the motte (or moat) and bailey type consisting of a large mound 50-100ft across the top, with steep sides and a ditch surrounding the base. On the top was a tower and, surrounding the ditch, a wall called a bailey. An example is Pen-maen old castle, a 12th century Norman defence, consisting of a massive circular stone bank of limestone, with a deep ditch to the front. When the area was excavated in 1961, traces of a large timbered gate tower were revealed. This had apparently been destroyed in an intense fire, and was not rebuilt. After the disaster the entrance was made narrower and a large stone hall was built on the seaward side of the site. Traces of the ditch and ramparts can still be seen.

The village of Pen-maen was once called Steadwarlango, which seems to have no trace of Welsh, and could possibly have been an old Scandinivian village. This village and church were completely buried by sand in the 14th century. Excavations in 1861 revealed the walls of a church. The church was a simple cell type and on the altar remained the fragments of a bronze censor representing a tower of the Heavenly

Rhosili Church

Scratch dial on left post of Rhosili Church

Jerusalem with the Holy Ghost hovering overhead in the shape of a dove. The discovery of this censor suggests that the church may have been abandoned in a hurry, perhaps during the Black Death when the church would have been abandoned and then covered by the encroaching sand.

Another motte and bailey type castle, Old Barland Castle, near Barland Common, is now only visible as mounds in the soil.

The Old Norman Penrice Castle is the largest in Gower, but contains few buildings. It is flanked by two large towers which are flat sided with rounded corners. Attached to the small round three storey keep, in the oldest part of the castle dating approximately to 1240, can be seen the remains of the hall. Today it is attractively overgrown with ivy. On the south east wall can be seen the well preserved stone Columbarium, or pigeon house, which was built around 1500.

Near the castle ruins, the road plunges steeply downhill. At the bottom, Penrice Mill was worked. This road is known by the delightful name of Penny Hitch. It dates back to a time when a man stood on the side of the road to hire out an extra horse to farmers who were struggling with a heavy load from the mill. The enterprising businessman would charge a penny for a hitch up the hill — hence the name.

Penrice Church was mentioned in the Confirmation of Bishop Anselm in 1230, and shows that the church and the lands were presented, between 1176 and 1198, to the preceptory of Slebach in Pembrokeshire, by Sir Robert de Penrice. Around 1330 the Church was supported by the Hospital of St David in Swansea, which was originally a house for aged priests and church laymen, now an Inn, and the oldest building in the City of Swansea. The chancel arch in the nave is of a Saxon design, and it is thought that the Normans must have employed a local Saxon mason.

Another of the mysteries of Gower is Pennard castle. Although no records exist, it is thought to have been built in the late 13th century and inhabited for only a very short time.

There is an old legend that the castle was erected overnight on the site of a stronghold built by the Danish rovers. The story goes that the castle was built by a Welsh sorcerer to save himself from the Normans, but surely a man capable of building a castle in one night could have fought off a few Normans.

Another tale relates that a well-known chief who was fond of fighting lived in the castle. It is said that he would help any Welsh ruler who needed assistance in battle. After winning a battle for one ruler, he was offered a reward, and asked for his daughter's hand in marriage. This

The Old Norman Penrice Castle

Pennard Castle

could not be refused, for it is said that twice he had saved the lord's life. The daughter, who knew of the chief's violent reputation, was at first saddened but was soon flattered when she realised how much he admired her. Elated at winning the battle and a wife, he returned to Pennard and threw a great feast. Soon the merriment was in full swing. The soldiers began singing and dancing, and it wasn't long before they became very drunk.

A sentry on guard on the castle wall heard strange sounds, and looked into the valley below. At first he must have thought he had drunk too much, for there on the grass he saw a flickering circle of light. Puzzled he stumbled down to the warden who, in a drunken stupor, was sitting in a corner chair by the fire. Finally he managed to rouse him, and together they watched as the flickering green patch danced before their eyes. Still puzzled, they ran to the hall and called the chief, who, thinking it was excuse for yet another battle, summoned his men to take up their swords. Fighting drunk, they staggered down the slope of the castle, and approached the grassy area. In the moonlight, they saw a group of fairies singing and dancing. The warriors burst into the ring brandishing their swords, but of course the fairies could only be seen and not touched. Suddenly a voice sounded: 'Unfortunate chief! Thou hast warrest against those that shall destroy thee. Thou hast wantonly spoiled our innocent sport and for that thy castle and township shall be destroyed.'

Suddenly it became cold, and the fairies vanished. Clouds of sand came swirling up the valley from the sea, filling the warriors' eyes, ears and mouths. The force of the gale sent the sand billowing over the houses and castle, until, within a few hours, everything was completely buried. It is also said that on that same evening a whole mountain of sand mysteriously disappeared from Ireland.

Like every good castle, Pennard has its ghost, the Gwrach-y-rhibyn. The spectre takes the form of the Irish banshee, a night hag. She has long black hair, sunken eyes, a crooked back, a thin figure, and flapping wings, and is seen wearing a black flowing robe. It is thought to be unlucky to sleep in the castle, and apparently one man who slept there was found unconscious with bruises on his body and deep facial cuts. On awaking he described a hag who 'clawed like an eagle and pecked at his body.' It is said that shortly after this incident he went insane.

One Norman Lord of Gower, William de Breose, was believed to have obtained the Lordship of Gower by blackmailing King John, threatening to drop out of the King's campaign in Normandy. Finally they fell out, and it is said that William fled to Normandy dying in poverty in 1212. William's wife Maud de St Valery, and his son were captured by King Maud refused to hand over her son as hostage to King John, and legend tells us that he had her and the boy walled up alive in a castle in Sussex. In December in the village of Bramber, near Steyning in Sussex, the ghosts of a child and a woman can be seen. They are either looking intently towards the ruined Bramber castle, which also belonged to the de Breose family, or begging in the main street. A Sussex legend says that they are the starved wife and son of William de Breose.

There is another story that during a feast William's grandson, another William de Breose, murdered Seisyllt, Prince of Gwent, and his followers. The story goes that William invited 70 Welsh guests to a feast and murdered them all. It was a deed that shocked the Welsh, and William was captured in battle by Llywelyn the Great, Prince of Gwynedd and North Wales. Whilst held prisoner William had an affair with Joan, Llywelyn's wife, daughter of King John. When Llywelyn heard of this he was furious and decided to play a trick on the Norman. He set William free and, to show that there were no hard feelings, invited him back to his castle. Once inside, he recaptured him, and hanged him from an oak tree, which tradition states, was the tree under which Joan and William would meet. We are not sure where he was hanged but some say it was at Aber in North Wales. Legend informs us that his body was brought back to Gower and buried in Cae Gwilym Ddu — Black William's Field, after the black-haired Norman, not far from Parc le Breos, on the original estate.

Another well known Norman family, the De la Mare's, are represented by two effigies in Gower. At Oxwich Church, in a tomb recess, on the north side of the chancel, lie the stone effigies of a Knight and His Lady. The Knight, who was a founder of the church, is clad in his mail-and-plate armour, and the Lady wears a flowing robe of the period with long sleeves and cuffs. Local legend states that they were descendants of the De la Mare family who occupied nearby Oxwich Castle at the time of the Norman Conquest. They are said to have drowned in the bay in the early part of the 1300s.

At Llangennydd church lies another member of the same family, seen as a crusader in chain-mail. Also buried in this Church is a Welsh Prince, Iestyn ap Gwrgan, showing that Welsh and Norman together shared a common faith, as well as a home in Gower.

CHAPTER FIVE

Medieval to Tudor Times

Wales moved into the 12th century with renewed confidence. The death of Henry I in 1135 was a sign for further hostile policies by the Welsh, but firmer actions by King Stephen held the promise of better defences in the future, although an attack on Gower in 1136 had its set-backs.

The first Welsh leader was Rhys ap Gruffydd, the grandson of Rhys ap Tudor, who later became known as Lord Rhys. Henry II, who reigned from 1154-89, recognised Lord Rhys's leadership skills and appointed him the King's Justiciar. When Rhys died, two Welsh princes, Llywelyn ab Iorwerth and Llywelyn Fawr, appeared on the scene. In 1282, when Llywelyn's grandson died in battle at Cilmeri near Builth, Wales came under the English crown, although Glamorgan, including Gower, had been under Norman rule since 1067.

Around this time an intriguing mystery of Gower was recorded in the Annals of Margam for 1185.

Opposite the Church of Llanrhidian, in a garden, is an ancient well known as St Illtyd's or Butter Well. It is recorded that one Thursday, a rich milk, instead of water, flowed from this well for three hours. People say that the milk coagulated and formed buttermilk around the sides, hence the name. The well never dries up, and although it is only a short distance away from the sea, at high tides the water is always fresh. The water is said to possess medicinal properties too, and jets up like a fountain, gurgling musically as it rises, before cascading down.

The unrest Gower was subjected to, including cross-channel traffic and settlers from the West Country, gave the peninsula its distinctive character. Small villages and the English system of open fields were introduced. Evidence of this, such as the viel at Rhosili remains. Even today fields are shared and worked between the farmers, just as in the Middle Ages.

Off Welsh Moor, near Llanelan Farm, there is reputed to be the lost medieval village and church of Llanelan. The exact position of the village is unknown, although it is said that only a few scattered stones, near a forgotten 500 year old yew tree remain. Records confirm its existence in the reign of Edward VI, but like any good Gower mystery, legend surrounds the loss of the village. A ship, returning from a crusade abroad, was wrecked in the Burry estuary and the survivors staggered ashore and climbed the steep hill to Llanelan. The villagers welcomed them with the usual warm hospitality of the Gower people, but unfortunately the ship's crew were carrying the deadly plague. Within a few days the entire village population had either been wiped out, or had fled in fear. Legend states that on the anniversary of the death of the village, the spirit of a lady, dressed in white, visits the area, weeping for the lost villagers. It is also a local tradition that to touch the stones or any remains of the village, is extremely unlucky. One farmer once took a stone from the area, but it rolled around with such fury that he was obliged to take it back.

By the reign of Henry IV, 1399-1413, a great leader Owain Glyndŵr, had emerged with several battle triumphs to his credit. By 1405 he had systematically destroyed all the castles in Gower. Like all good folk heroes Owain Glyndŵr is shrouded in mystery. We know he was descended from Welsh princes and that he became a law student at the Inns of Court in London, but by about 1412 he had disappeared. No-one knows how or when he died.

Harsh laws were imposed on the Welsh, but finally in 1485, Harri Tudor, a Welshman, born in Pembroke Castle, became Henry VII, King of England. The English saw this as a 'War of the Roses' triumph, with the House of Lancaster gaining over the House of York. But the Welsh had something to celebrate too. Not only was Henry born in Wales, but he was nursed by a Welsh foster-mother, and most probably could speak the native language.

King Henry granted the Lordship of Gower to his uncle, Jasper Tudor, and by 1536 Henry VIII had passed an act incorporating Wales into the English Dominions. Following the Dissolution of the Monasteries and the general unrest, many Welsh foundations were destroyed, and most of the manor houses such as Weobley Castle, which is not a real castle but a fortified manor house, began to protect themselves against attack.

When Owain Glyndŵr raided Gower, Weobley Castle, which was built in the 13th century by Henry Beaufort, Duke of Warwick, was occupied by Sir John de la Bere. It then passed into the hands of Sir Rhys ap Thomas, who was a courtier to Henry II. During the reign of Henry VIII, the castle was given to Catherine Edgecombe. When Lady Catherine died in 1547, it was leased to Sir William Herbert. Ten years later Anthony

Mansel of Llanrithid purchased the castle. It remained in the Mansel family for many generations, until it was finally handed over to the Ministry of Works in 1911. It is an interesting castle because some of the towers have six or eight sides, whilst others are square. All join to make a complete square.

Oxwich Castle, which was actually a court-yard house, was built by Sir Rice Mansel on the site of the ruined Oxwich 'old' Castle, home of the Norman de la Mare family in the 13th and 14th centuries. The house was built around a courtyard in a mock military design to represent the new powerful Tudor gentry that were emerging. The courtyard was entered through a stone gateway. Inside the courtyard two buildings stand side by side. They appear to be independent of each other and could have accommodated two separate households. Until recent years the smaller two storey block was occupied as a farmhouse. Sir Rice also had interests in Beaupre, near Cowbridge, and, later, Margam. It would appear that Oxwich Castle was built in an early phase of his career. Who knows? He may have been thinking of it as an ancestral home for his descendants.

The dovecote at the north end of the site may have been built in Sir Rice Mansel's time. Pigeons were kept in the columbarium by most households during this period. They would have provided the family with food during the seasons when supplies of fresh meat were difficult to obtain.

The much larger east end of the castle is an independent Great House and designed in a complex way. It was built between 1559-80, and would have stretched even the most lavish of budgets. Records show that Sir Mansel had some financial difficulties in the 1560s. Maybe the building of this magnificent mansion house was the cause. Steps lead from the porch to a large first floor hall, and above, the windows of the long gallery can still be seen today. The Long Gallery was often a room distant from the Great Hall for exercise in wet weather to stave off constipation! A number of chambers in the three towers provided ample accommodation for the family, as well as the large army of servants needed for such a residence.

In 1968 a gold ring brooch was discovered at Oxwich Castle. It was assumed that it was a heirloom of the Mansel family, but it has also been suggested that it had once formed part of Edward II's treasure, some of which was dispersed from Swansea Castle in about 1326. Today the brooch can be seen in the National Museum of Wales.

During the 16th century, around 1560-70, enterprising trespassers began to take over the open neglected waste lands around Gower, fence

Oxwich Castle

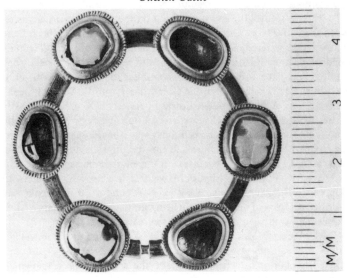

The Ring Brooch found at Oxwich Castle

them in, and start farming. These were mainly estates that belonged to the Earls of Worcester, the hereditary marcher Lords of Gower, and in 1684 an enclosure of some 282 acres of the moor in Penrice was achieved. This continued until the whole of the common disappeared. Soon Gower began to expand and prosper as these farms were enlarged, and tenants were finally granted the 'liberty to enclose and manure.' West Gower became known as 'South Gowerland'. Rhosili at this time was known as 'all corn ground'.

North and South Gower had two distinct dialects. Edward Lhuyd, who pioneered studies into the Celtic language and was keeper at the Ashmolean Museum at Oxford in 1696, wrote that the inhabitants of south Gower, known as Gower Anglicana, which included Oxwich and Port Einion, ' . . . did pronounce their words something like the West of England'. In the North, known as Gower Wallicana, which included the villages of Cheriton and Llanrhidian, the inhabitants were 'more inclined to the Welsh and mixed some Welsh words amongst their 'Old English'. This mix of dialect is not surprising when you consider the past; the divide is still in evidence today, and North Gower residents are still Welsh speaking.

The imposing ruined Oystermouth castle that is seen today dates from the 13th and 14th centuries. It was built on the site of an earlier castle, established in 1100. This was burnt by the Welsh in 1116 and the occupants slaughtered, although it is believed that the owner, William de Londres, fled. The Castle was rebuilt, only to be burned down exactly one hundred years later in 1216. Warfare continued to plague the castle until the death in 1282 of Llywelyn the Great, the last of the Welsh Princes. During a tour of Wales in 1284, Edward I stayed at Oystermouth Castle for two days, but a couple of years later an uprising destroyed the castle again. The square keep that is seen today was damaged at this time, but was repaired when the gatehouse and the curtain walls were built a few years later. As the castle at Swansea became more important, the role of Oystermouth became less significant so that it caused no problem to Cromwell during the English Civil War. Around 1650 the castle was described as: 'An old decayed castle being for the present of noe use, but of a pleasant scituacon and near unto the sea side'.

Nearby Pickett's Mead, however takes its name from the Cromwellian period. It is said that Cromwell, on his way to the siege at Pembroke, picketed his horses in a field there, and the name has been known as Pickett's Mead ever since.

CHAPTER SIX

Some Famous Gower Families

No story of Gower would be complete without a mention of some of the well known local families, and the colourful tales that surround them.

The Lucas family have been living in the Gower Peninsula for at least 500 years. Geoffrey, the first Lucas, came from Essex around 1450 and married Anne Mansel of Henllys. This was the first of many marriages between the two families. Their son, also Geoffrey, married Mary Craddock of Cheriton, and their grandson, David, married Isobel Baker of Nicholson Hall.

One of David's children, John, left the family home in Reynoldston to found the infamous line of the Salthouse Lucases. He was probably born around 1510, and was thought to have been the eldest son. Why he did not inherit his father's home in Reynoldston is uncertain. It may have been due to a family quarrel. John was a lovable character, a rover who had spent nine years ' . . . adventuring and soldiering'. On his return to Gower, his father built him a mansion called Salthouse, and he married Jane Grove a local girl. Perhaps the Salthouse was a bribe to encourage the swashbuckling John to settle down to married bliss. If so, then it didn't work.

Immediately John fortified the mansion. With George ab Eynon, Robert de Scurlage and the Mansels of Henllys, he became a wrecker of ships and smuggled contraband. Although he was a violent man, he always shared his spoils with the village folk — a sort of Gowerian Robin Hood — and maintained the poor of the village. It is thought that the Gilbert and Sullivan opera *The Pirates of Penzance* is based on John's notorious adventures. With so many ships grounded around the Gower coast, we can assume that the cellars of the Salthouse would have been bursting with illicit goodies. Some say that John passed on a very profitable piracy business to his son Philip. Others claim that in later life he settled down, abandoned his unlawful activities, and partly dismantled the defences of the Salthouse.

The mansion remained in the Lucas family for seven generations, and the last Lucas to live there, also John, eventually brought a legal industry to Port Einion. He discovered that if the iron stained shales of millstone were pounded into particles, they produced minerals which were useful in the making of paint. Two colours were produced, a dark red and black. Later when a Mr Talbot became a director of the Great Western Railway, he insisted the company use the paint supplied by Port Einion on all their railway carriages and good wagons. The practice continued until Mr Talbot retired. The paint making trade thrived until in 1703 a great storm flooded the Salthouse and destroyed John Lucas's small fleet of ships. It is said that he was so upset at the loss of his home and business that he died of a broken heart. He is reputed to be buried at Sedger's Bank, which is now a nature reserve.

One of the great curiosities of Gower is a tall narrow cleft in the rock beyond Port Einion point, known as Culver Hole. It is thought to have been either a smuggler's hideout, or a pigeon house. Could this have been a stronghold built by the notorious John Lucas? Or could it have been a giant pigeon loft for the Salthouse? There is also a story that there is a secret passage between the Salthouse and Culver Hole, although this has never been discovered. This could have been used for transporting illicit goods to the Salthouse. Or was it simply a passageway for the servants to the pigeon house? Whatever it was, the walls were 10ft thick with no provision made inside for floors, although there is a crude stone staircase along the inner face of the wall.

During 1770, there was a riot at Cheriton Church between the two branches of the Lucas family. Apparently it was over some land in the manor of Llandimore, part of Cheriton. The rivals were John Lucas the elder, of the Stouthall branch and his two cousins, also called John. They were father and son of the Salthouse branch of the family, who, after the storm of 1703, were living at the Great House in Horton. The Rector of Cheriton, Rev. John Williams, was locked in his church by the crowd, 'it being offensive to shed blood in the sight of the Clergy.' His daughter, Anne, was related to both parties and decided not to take sides. She watched the fighting from the window of her father's residence, the Great House at Cherrytown, this being the old name for Cheriton because of its abundance of cherry trees. One of the Cheriton inhabitants was killed in the fight.

Another well known Gower family, the Mansels once lived in Penrice Castle, but during the first half of the 16th century they abandoned it to

The Old Salthouse home of John Lucas at Port Einion

The Church at Cheriton

live in their newly built Oxwich Castle. You can still see the impressive Mansel crest above the gateway which leads to the courtyard. It was under this very gateway that tragedy struck the family on 28th December 1557.

Sir George Herbert, of Swansea, was Vice-Admiral of the Crown and heard that a French ship had been wrecked off the Oxwich coast. Being a leading citizen of Swansea, he considered that he had legal rights to the cargo, and therefore had more claim to the pickings than the inhabitants of Oxwich. Sir George rode to the area to claim the spoils. Meanwhile the crew had been taken prisoner and the cargo removed and divided between the Mansel family and the local villagers. Angrily he rode over to Oxwich castle to try and reason with Sir Rice Mansel and his son Edward. They were both out so Sir George took three of the French prisoners with him. He concluded that they should ransack the cottages and store the booty in the church, until the villagers reached some sort of an agreement.

Edward, meanwhile was visiting his aunt, Anne, at nearby Llanddewi. Sir George and his men decided to await his return. News of the incident had by now reached Edward, and Anne fearing that there would be a fight, chose to ride along and act as a peacemaker. Edward and his men stood defiantly on either side of the gateway. Anne joined her nephew's side in the centre, appealing to the crowd, and hoping that the presence of a woman would calm the two parties down. Tempers became short and a fight broke out. One of Sir George's followers threw a stone at the Mansel crowd and it struck Anne on the forehead. As she collapsed with blood pouring from the wound, a cry of "Murder! Murder!" rang out from the Mansel crowd. Realising what had happened Sir George quickly withdrew his men and made a hasty retreat to Swansea. A few days later Anne Mansel died from her wounds. The case went to court and Sir George Herbert was found guilty, fined heavily, and made to return the goods to the people of Oxwich.

Another well known Gower family were the Aces, but none were quite so famous as Jessie and Margaret Ace, the daughters of Abraham Ace, who was the lighthouse keeper at Mumbles during the 1880s.

One blustery night in January 1883, a Prussian barge, the Admiral Prinz Adelbert of Danzig, crashed into the rocks off Mumbles Head. The lifeboat, 'Wolverhampton', was launched and the crew battled with the elements to reach the stricken vessel. However the waves were fierce, the lifeboat was flung against the wreck and four of the crew were lost. Coxswain Jenkins lost two of his sons and a son-in-law in the disaster. Four women were widowed and fourteen children orphaned. Two crewmen were saved thanks to the Ace sisters who, seeing the disaster from a window, rushed down to the water's edge. They knotted their shawls together and threw them to the drowning men. With their father and gunner Edward Hutchings, they hauled the two men to safety. The story hit the headlines, touched the hearts of the whole nation and is immortalised in a ballad written by the famous Victorian writer, Clement Scott, and entitled 'The Women of Mumbles Head'. It was popularly recited as part of the music halls acts of the day.

The Jenkins brothers were buried in Oystermouth Church where their gravestones can still be seen. A brass plaque on the north west wall records that the window near the pulpit was erected to the memory of the four men of the Mumbles Lifeboat 'Wolverhampton' who lost their lives on the 27th January 1883. The window depicts the figure of Christ in the upper half and in the lower panel is the Mumbles Lifeboat propelled by oars as would have been the case in 1883.

The Women of Mumbles Head

Bring novelists, your notebook! bring dramatists your pen!
And I'll tell you a single story of what women do for men.
It's only a tale of a lifeboat, of the dying and the dead.
Of a terrible storm and shipwreck, that happened off Mumbles Head.
Maybe you have travelled in Wales, sir, and know it north and south;
Maybe you are friends with the natives that dwell at Oystermouth;
It happened, no doubt, that from Bristol you've crossed in a casual way
And have sailed your yacht in the summer, in the blue of Swansea bay.

Well, it isn't like that in the winter, when the lighthouse stands alone,
In the teeth of Atlantic breakers, that foam on its face of stone,
It wasn't like that when the hurricane blew, and storm bells tolled or when
There was news of a wreck, and the life-boat, and a desperate cry for men.
When in the work did the coxswain shirk? a brave salt was he!
Proud to the bone of as four strong lad as ever had tasted the sea,
Welshmen all to the lungs and loins, who, about the coast 'twas said,
Had saved some hundred lives a piece — at a shilling or so a head!

It didn't go well with the lifeboat! 'twas a terrible storm that blew,
And it snapped the rope in a second that was flung to the drowning crew;
And then the anchor parted — 'twas a tussle to keep afloat!
But the father stuck to the rudder, and the boys to the brave old boat.

Then at last on the poor doom'd lifeboat a wave broke mountains high!
'God help us now!' said the father, 'it's over my lads goodbye'.
Half the crew swam seawards! half to the sheltered caves,
But father and sons were fighting death in the foam of the angry waves.

Up at the lighthouse window two women beheld the storm.
And saw in the boiling breakers a figure — a fighting form,
It might be a grey haired father, then the women held their breath,
It might be a fair haired brother, who was having a round with death,
It might be a lover, a husband whose kisses were on the lips
Of the women whose love is the life of men, going down to the sea in ships:
They had seen the launch of the lifeboat, then had seen the worst and more;
Then kissing each other, these women went down from the lighthouse straight
to the shore.

There by the rocks on the breakers these sisters, hand in hand,
Beheld once more that desperate man who struggled to the reach the land.
'Twas only aid he wanted to help him across the wave
But what are a couple of women with only a man to save?
What are a couple of women? well more than three craven men
Who stood by the shore with chattering teeth refusing to stir — and then
Off went the women's shawls, sir, in a second they're torn and rent,
Then knotting them into a rope of love, straight into the sea they went!

'Come back!' cried the lighthouse keeper, 'For God's sake girls, come back!'
As they caught the waves on their foreheads, resisting the fierce attack.
'Come back!' moaned the grey haired mother, as she stood by the angry sea,
'If the waves take you, my darlings, there's nobody left to me.'
'Come back!' said the three strong soldiers. who still stood faint and pale.
'You'll drown in the face of the breakers! You will fall if you brave the gale!'
'Come back!' said the girls, 'we will not! go tell it to all the town
We'll lose our lives, God willing, before that man shall drown'.

'Give one more knot to the shawls, Bess! Give one strong clutch of your hand!
Just follow me, brave, to the shingle, and we'll bring him safe to land!
Wait for the next wave, daring, only a minute more,
And I'll have him safe in my arms, dear, and we'll drag him safe to the shore.'
Up to the arms in water, fighting it breast to breast,
They caught and saved a brother alive! God bless us we know the rest —
Well many a heart beats stronger, and many a tear was shed,
And many a glass was tossed right off to the Women of Mumbles Head.

Another well known character of the Ace family, Betty Ace, lived in Rhosili and was nicknamed the 'Doctoress'. For about forty years, Betty acted as the village's unqualified doctor. She could be seen clambering over the rocks, or hunting the hedgerows for herbs, which she boiled, steamed and crushed to make into her ointments and medicines. It is said that, 'what Betty Ace didn't know about humans and beasts wasn't worth knowing.'

There is a tale that has been told around many a glowing fire in Gower about a fight between Betty and another resident, Sarah Bowen. The women of Rhosili used to make laverbread (called 'Iowa' locally), which involved picking the seaweed, boiling it and then chopping it finely with a meat cleaver. The women didn't have a fixed pitch, but there was one spot, in the middle of Rhosili Bay, called the Cow and Calf, not exposed today, which produced this weed in abundance. The pickers always rushed to be the first at this spot, and one day it seems that the 'Doctoress' must have got there before Sarah. A fight began, a huge crowd gathered, and someone in the village wrote a verse about it, which has been handed down for the last hundred years or more. It goes like this:

There was a mighty battle
Fought on Rhossil sands
Between the Queen of Sheba (Sarah)
And the Doctoress of our land.
The Doctoress's name was Betty
She was a savage race,
She wore a dreadful counteance,
The daughter of Sam Ace.
The Queen was tall and fiery
And fought like Higgie's cat
But what she gained in inches
Was lost by too much fat.
The Doctoress poked and parried,
The Queen she used her nails,
The battle raged with fury
As each the other shook,
The Doctoress punched the harder,
But Sheba used her hook.
So when the contest ended

'Twas fairly plain to see
That neither had asked for mercy:
For one was buying plaster,
And t'other couldn't see.

CHAPTER SEVEN

Legal Trading in Gower

One of the oldest industries in Gower is farming, which we know was carried out in the Neolithic period. Not far behind must be the cockle and oyster-catching industries. Although their origins are obscure, it is certain that both date back to prehistoric times.

The cockle industry is mainly found in Pen-clawdd. These small creatures were picked by tough women who would wait for the tide to ebb before riding out to the sandy seabed to collect their harvest before they could be trapped between the flowing streams or 'pills' that cascade down from the Gower Hills.

In 43 A.D. the Romans invaded Britain and fierce fighting with the Welsh tribes resulted. A garrison occupied the city of Loughor in North Gower, and this army had to be fed. It was up to the 'Women of the Sands' to play their part by providing fresh food for the troops. It meant working these cockle beds every time the tide went out. Children started work at a very early age, and although it was too dangerous for them to be out in the bay, they were employed collecting fuel for the fires that heated the cauldrons used for cooking the cockles. The Roman Legions occupied the area for almost 400 years.

During one of the peak periods of the industry, in the late 1940s, as many as sixty-three tons of cockles were gathered each week. Although some men worked the beds, the majority of the gatherers were still women. They would line up, some driving ponies and carts, others side saddle on small donkeys, buckets and sacks strapped to their waists, with shawls over their heads tied by a band round their temples. Black worsted stockings would provide warmth, although the feet were cut away and open sandals offered little protection from the winds. As the tide ebbed the convoy would ride out across the sand, and the sound of hymns and arias would resound from 200 or more Welsh voices as they harmonised to the rhythm of the clattering hooves of the animals. Little wonder these women were called the 'Welsh nightingales'. During the winter months they suffered great hardship as biting westerly gales froze their fingers. In these conditions they resembled a horde of Bedouin tribesmen battling against a sandstorm.

Although times have changed, the method of gathering is still the same as in pre-Roman times. It is a back breaking task, and the women work in pairs, one clearing the mud with a knife or 'scrap' to expose the cockles, the other gathering them into a large cockle sieve.

Today the sieve must conform to size to allow the smaller cockles to fall out thus allowing only those of about five to six years old to be gathered. The age of a cockle can be assessed by the number of rings on the shell i.e. two in its first year, and one each year thereafter. The process of scraping, sieving, washing and shaking the cockles continues until a complete load is gathered. These are then taken to one of several factories dotted around Penclawdd where the process of removing the molluscs from the shells is now made easy by automation. Heat is provided by gas cylinders and large stainless steel urns can boil 2½ cwt of cockles. After heating, the open shells are tipped into a rotating wire mesh cylinder that is angled to allow them to roll down a chute and form piles of empty shells in the yard outside. These are finally ground into different grades of grit and sold to poultry farmers for mixing with chicken feed. The cockles roll into shallow trays and are washed, up to six times, in clean water, before being considered clean enough to be bagged and sent to market. Here a familiar cry would be 'COCOS HEDDIW COCOS' — Cockles, today, cockles.

In days gone by, the women would walk barefoot, with tubs on their heads and baskets strapped to their waists, to Swansea market, a distance of ten miles. On the way they would stop at a brook called 'Yr Olchfa' (The Wash House), to wash their feet and put on boots to be respectable on entering Swansea.

The age of steam made life easier for the gatherers and provided a colourful scene at Penclawdd on a Saturday morning. The women would be seen, dressed in their traditional costumes, chattering in Welsh, and filling the length of the platform. The two-thirty train arriving from Swansea was nicknamed 'The Relish', by the men of Penclawdd, because, after a day in the market, the womenfolk would bring back some tasty delights for supper. The typical dress of the day was a red and white striped dress, a black and white checked apron, with a Welsh flannel shawl, made locally, wrapped around the shoulders. The hat was not the tall variety that is associated with Wales, but a flat tight fitting black hat, called a 'cockle hat'.

Cockle Women going to market

Cockles are gathered from Monday to Friday, boiled the same day and sold the following morning. It is illegal to gather cockles on a Sunday, and any purchased on a Monday are therefore not freshly picked. Although the industry is still alive, it no longer attracts the youngsters of the village. Unless the situation can be reversed, it appears that a tradition that has survived for centuries is dwindling.

Another industry that probably dates back to the Roman times is oyster catching. The seventeenth century was perhaps the peak of the oyster industry's success. This is confirmed in an account of the official progress of His Grace, Henry, 1st Duke of Beaufort, Lord President of the Council in Wales and Lord Warden of the Marches. His Grace visited Swansea on 16th August 1684, and the streets were strewn with fresh sand for his progress. He wrote: 'In view of this Harbour of Swansea is Oystermouth sayd to be the best bed of Oysters in Great Britain'. A survey at the time confirms the Duke's views.

By 1809, twenty-five large open boats each with a single sail operated from Oystermouth. By 1880s, when dredging was at its height, there were nearly 200 oyster ketches. However, by 1920-21, a disease among the oysters finished the trade for good.

In the 19th century oyster fishing was also one of the main industries in Port Einion, and between 1830 and 1850, there were up to forty skiffs operating out of Port Einion. The oystermen would assemble on the beach at dawn each day in winter to discuss the weather signs, and to take a majority vote on whether to embark on a trip. These conferences were known locally as 'makin almanacks'. Although precautions were taken disasters often occurred. One particular morning in 1851, four skippers assembled on the beach, but, owing to bad weather, their crews failed to show up, so the skippers decided to go together in one skiff. Henry Chalk of Port Einion, James Rees of Kitehole, William Janes of Horton and John Jenkins of Slade perished off Slade's Foot. In 1870 William Horwood lost his life when his leg caught on a coil of rope and he was pulled under the skiff.

Despite the risks it was a profitable trade. In the early 19th century the oystermen would receive one penny for two dozen oysters, rising in price until they fetched nearly one penny each in the 1870s.

Today, just past the youth hostel, is an area known as Crowder's Quay, where the oyster catches were landed. The oysters were stored in 'perched pools,' a portion of the foreshore that was marked off by lines of stone. From there the oysters were transferred by fishing smack to Bristol and

Swansea, and then by steam packet, to more distant ports. In the 18th century, on the ruins of the old Salthouse, two cottages were built for the families who worked the oyster beds. These were inhabited by them for some 150 years. In 1710, Hugh Clement, who owned a vessel which operated from Port Einion, and also acted as bailiff to the Lord of the manor, lived in one of the cottages. The oyster season lasted from September to early March, and in the summer months the men worked in Port Einion's other main industry, limestone quarrying.

The quarry still mars the hillside and stands as a permanent reminder of how important it was for the life of the village. The limestone was brought down to the shore by cart, and at low tide stacked into two parallel lines. To the west of the bay a wooden pole marked the centre, and can still be seen today. When the tide came in boats, mainly from Bideford and Barnstaple, would anchor seawards and row in, guided by the pole until abreast of the stones. As the tide receded the boat was left aground and all hands, including families of the Port Einion men involved, would turn out to load the stone. On the next tide the boat would be pulled out to the deep water by a winch, which was hauled on the anchor cable, and refloated on the flood. To stabilize the empty ships on the return journey, the Devonshire men would use their own local distinctive blue-green coloured stone, which they would discard on the beach after each trip. Today these alien stones can be seen adding a tinge of colour to the landscape.

Llanrhidian, and Cheriton are famous for the traditional craft of weaving, which was still a thriving trade at the beginning of this century. In the lower village of Llanrhidian can be found a three storey building alongside a large pond. This is Nether Mill. On the wall below the chimney you will see a slate plaque which reads:

> *'BUILT IN THE YEAR 1803*
> *AT THE SOLE EXPENSE OF WM.M. EVANS'*

Masons	*Carpenters*
John Beynon	*William Edwards*
Evan Jenkins	*George Evans*

Not far from Nether Mill, at the end of the road, are the former buildings of the woollen factory called Stavel Hagar. The looms, which were dismantled in 1904 when Richard Dix left the parish, were driven by a water-wheel and water taken from the river at a point near to the church stile.

Richard's father Joseph took over the business from his father when he brought Mary, his young bride from Cheriton. Mary learnt the art of dyeing the yarns, and as more colours were discovered, so the number of spools on Joseph's loom increased. By the time Richard Dix took over, quilts and bedspreads were woven to a very high standard. Minka, a coarse striped flannel, well known for its hard wearing qualities was produced at this mill as well as Tanner's Mill at Cheriton. I am sure there are many oak chests in farms and cottages in Gower today that contain samples of the weavers' handiwork.

The employees, like most Gowerians, wore the traditional Gower whittle, or red shawl, made in the 18th century by George Dix, great grandfather to Richard Dix. In days gone by this would have been fastened with a blackthorn which, when dried, was strong enough to penetrate the coarse material. The family continued to live at Stavel Hagar until 1950 when Harriet Dix, the last link with the weaving industry, passed away.

With such a wild and rugged coastline, seamanship was naturally a strong feature of Gower trades. This was especially true at Port Einion which, although noted as a shipping graveyard, was not given a lifeboat until a steamship was wrecked.

The incident involved the 'Agnes Jack' of Liverpool, which was carrying a cargo of lead ore from Swansea to Llanelli on the same night that the Mumbles lifeboat was assisting the 'Admiral Prinz Adalbert' in trouble at Mumbles Head. Because of bad weather, the 'Agnes Jack' had been sheltering in Swansea Bay. She sailed on the evening tide of 27th February, 1883, but soon after leaving the safe haven of the Bay ran into a westerly gale. She took in a large amount of water which eventually put her boilers out and was driven ashore in the early hours of the morning of the 28th near Port Einion Point. By first light only the mast, with twenty-one people — twenty crew and one passenger — clinging desparately to it, could be seen above the water. The lifeboat teams from Oxwich and Rhossili arrived. Their lines were too short to reach the wreck, so they decided to wait for low tide. This proved fatal as the force of the waves eventually snapped the mast throwing everyone into the sea.

After the disaster the RNLI decided to form a lifeboat station at Port Einion. A building was erected and the first lifeboat, 'A Daughter's Offering', was provided from the bequest of £1,000 from a Miss Maria Jones of Liverpool. Launched on 10 May, 1884, it was a ten-oared 34ft self-righting boat. It was not called into service until 13 January 1885

Nether Mill at Llanrhidian

when it went to the assistance of the Hull steamship, 'Milan', bound from Alexandria to Bristol with a cargo of cottonseed.

In July 1906 a new 35ft self righting lifeboat, designed to be launched in the shallow waters of the Bay, was installed. Named 'Janet', she first saw service on 22 December 1909 when she was called to the aid of a French steamship, 'Lutec', stranded at Southgate.

On 1 January, 1916, tragedy struck 'Janet' when she was launched to assist the Glasgow steamship 'Dunregan', which had run aground at Oxwich. Because of the strong gale and large breakers around the crippled ship, the lifeboat was unable to assist. Rocket apparatus was set up as a signal or landmark on the nearby cliffland to enable 'Janet' and the crew to make for port. Its lifeboat capsized twice and the crew were thrown into the water. Coxswain William Gibbs, Second Coxswain William Eynon, and lifeboatman George Harry were found to be missing. Because of the distress this disaster caused, Port Einion lifeboat station was closed. The 'Janet' was sent to Stornoway in the Hebrides for the remainder of her service.

Today, overlooking the road, proudly stands the white marble figure of Coxswain William Gibbs, erected in the churchyard to commemorate the bravery and devotion of the men who lost their lives on that tragic day in 1916.

Memorial erected for the lifeboat disaster 1st Jan 1916

CHAPTER EIGHT

Illegal Activities in Gower

The name Brandy Cove conjures up a world of illicit smuggling. The secluded cove, originally called Hareslade, was renamed during the Napoleonic Wars, when it became a smugglers' paradise.

One of Gower's famous smugglers was a Devonshire man called William Arthur, who lived at Great Highway farm, less than a mile from Brandy Cove. The Arthurs operated along the coast as far as Oxwich. They hired about one hundred men and because they paid them far more than the average farm labourer in Gower, they were never short of help. It seems everyone was involved whether they wanted to be or not. Horses were 'borrowed' from the farmers who did not seem to complain, providing a keg or two of brandy paid for their help. As brandy could be purchased in France for £1 a four gallon cask, profits were considerable and it was well worth taking a few risks.

One cold January day in 1786 customs men at Swansea were tipped off that a French ship was due to discharge its cargo that afternoon. They had been trying to capture William and his gang for some time and decided to lie in wait and catch them red handed. By evening William's men had moved all the goods to the undiscovered cellars near Great Highway Farm. The customs men, about twenty in all, waited until after dark and then knocked on the door of the farm. Finding it in total darkness, they knocked harder until finally a sleepy voice told them to go away. Suddenly the door flew open and the masked gang rushed out, beat the customs men and rolled them in the farmyard muck. In a sorry state, and with the shouts of delight from the smugglers ringing in their ears, they retreated. For a while, the smugglers were able to work unhindered in broad daylight.

On another occasion, the customs men arrived at Great Highway Farm with a search warrant, and after a while a keg of spirits was discovered in the loft. The Chief Officer, having experienced this notorious gang evading arrest, sat firmly on the contraband to prevent the smugglers

Brandy Cove where the smugglers landed illicit goods

Worm's Head scene of the Wreckers

taking it with them, whilst his assistant fetched a horse. William immediately arranged for his men to make as much noise as possible outside the loft. In the room below, a hole was drilled through the wooden ceiling and into the keg of spirits. Carefully they siphoned off the spirit, and the officer was left sitting on an empty keg. Without the evidence, the gang could not be arrested.

In 1804, an observant customs officer noticed a strange unevenness in the earthen floor of the kitchen and decided to investigate. The soil was removed and a trap-door leading to a secret cellar well stocked with smuggled spirits, was revealed. A thorough search found a similar cellar beneath the barn, and the customs men finally took possession of some 3,000 gallons of spirits.

An extract from the diary of John Collins, Rector of Oxwich Church from 1771-1814, clearly shows the effect the smuggling trade had on the inhabitants of Gower:

'Thursday 13 March 1794. Smugglers were chased by the Speedwell Cutter, and some casks of liquor were saved, but several parishioners got very drunk.'

With tragic results it seems, as on Saturday 15 March the entry states that 'Thomas Matthews died owing to drinking a quantity of gin,' and on Sunday 16th 'Buried Matthews, 200 people attended.'

I think Rudyard Kipling, summed up the secrecy of the smuggling business in his famous poem, *Traders in the Night*.

If you wake at midnight, and hear a horse's feet,
Don't go drawing back the blind, or looking in the street,
Them that ask no questions isn't told a lie,
Watch the wall, my darling, while the Gentlemen go by!

> Five and twenty ponies
> Trotting through the dark —
> Brandy for the Parson,
> Baccy for the Clerk,
> Laces for a lady, letters for a spy,

And watch the wall, my darling, while the Gentlemen go by!

Most pubs in Gower will recall the tale of Moses Gibb, an oysterman who died in 1765. One winter's day Moses was dredging with the Port Einion fleet in the Channel when he spotted a French lugger, with a cargo of illicit brandy on board, anchored in the bay. Suddenly Moses noticed the Revenue cutter making its way up the West Coast, and alerted the captain, Barneo Farneaux. As the cutter rounded Port Einion point, he managed to slip his cable and head for the safer waters in the South East. The Captain dropped a keg of spirit overboard as a thank-you for Moses, who managed to recover it, and headed for the bay at speed. The cutter gave chase, but the Frenchman was quicker and eventually lost to the distant horizon.

Another story concerns Mollie Stote, wife of one of the Rhosili gang of smugglers. One hot summer's day, suspecting that the Stotes were involved in smuggling, the customs men arrived at her cottage in Middleton to question her. Mrs Stote knew a consignment of brandy was sitting in the barn. When the officials said they were hot, she seized the opportunity to confuse them. Smiling sweetly she offered them a drink of water, filling the glasses with neat gin! They downed it, and Mollie quickly refilled the empty glasses. It was not long before the men slid to the floor in a drunken stupor. Mollie was able to call her husband and, with the rest of the gang, they moved the casks to safety.

During the 17th and 18th centuries, gangs of workers called Wreckers ran many lucrative businesses off the coast of Rhosili beach, which was known locally as the 'Wreckers Coast'. They earned a living by luring ships up the Channel, past Lundy, towards Worms Head where the ships would be pounded to pieces on the rocks. Any unsuspecting captain peering out into the darkness would see a light, which they would assume was a safe port. The 'safe port' often turned out to be a mule or a child walking back and forth along the cliff edge with a lantern hung on a cow's horn to simulate a ship heading for port. Many ships were driven onto the rocks in this way and, to prevent survivors telling the true happenings of the night, they were usually murdered.

A Spanish ship, the *El Dorado*, was wrecked around 1660-1690, although the exact date and location is unknown. It has became known locally as the *Dollar Ship* because it was carrying dollars and pieces of eight. It was rumoured to be one of three vessels filled with treasure to form the dowry of a Spanish princess who had been, or was about to be, married to an English nobleman. Two vessels were lost and one reached safety. Another wreck further along the coast at Bluepool Bay, near Broughton, in the parish of Llangennydd, may give us a clue to its identity. Here gold moidores were found, and as these are Portuguese coins, the wreck is thought to be Portuguese. This ship is often confused with the *Dollar Ship*, but perhaps the two vessels perished together?

A letter dated 21st March 1697 from an agent called Alexander Trotter to Sir Edward Mansel, mentions duty payable on iron salvaged from a Spanish ship. Only half the iron was recovered owing to difficulties with the salvaging operation. The letter may help us date the wreck. Perhaps the ship had been wrecked in 1690 and remained submerged until the tidal conditions made it possible to attempt a recovery operation? The wreck at Bluepool Bay must have occurred in the late 17th century as moidores were Portuguese coins that were minted between 1690-1722.

Even more intriguing is the theory that this could have been a ship carrying Catherine of Braganza's dowry. We know Catherine arrived safely on our shores but no mention has been made about a dowry to Charles II. A few years after her marriage, a Mr Mann reported in state papers dated 1666, a wreck of a 'Phyal vessel ladened with wine, sugar and Brazil wood on sands 10 miles off Swansea. The men are Portuguese and cannot speak English, hoped to have saved the vessel and refused to save the goods, so all was lost.'

Mansel of Henllys, who lived at nearby Llanddewi, was thought to have been the leader of the wreckers and confiscated most of the treasure from the *El Dorado*. On the night of the sinking he himself mysteriously disappeared. Local legend states that he fled the country, but did he really take the ship's treasure and run? Perhaps he was murdered for his newly acquired wealth. Some believe that his ghost still haunts the bay, racing across the sand in a black coach pulled by four grey mares.

It seems that most of the Rhosili people, were at one time involved in the lucrative business of wrecking — even the clergy! It is recorded that one preacher, who often prayed for the safety of the sailors, was always aware of his parishioners needs too. 'But', he would pray, 'If it be thy will that they be cast away, send them ashore here Lord, and not amongst the wicked in the next parish.'

One of the best documented incidents occurred in 1712. It made such an impression on the people that it is preserved in ballad form by Dr J. M. Neale (1818-1866), a scholar and hymnologist. There are various versions told around the glowing firesides of Gower, but the most accurate account is as follows:

On Easter Day 1712, the coast of Gower was lashed with violent storms which gave the wreckers an ideal opportunity to perform their evil deeds. In the evening they gathered at the Goat Inn, now disappeared, to plan their evening's activities. A fourteen year old orphan girl called Kate had been sent to work for these wreckers, in return for her keep. She was poorly dressed, and often treated cruelly. Her task was to carry a lantern backwards and forwards across the cliffs. To her it was a night's work, which provided her with a roof and a meal. It is reported that she remained unmoved by the sounds of the crashing timbers and the screams of the sailors as their ships hit the rocks. Although illiterate, she was allowed to attend church, and could repeat the Creed and The Lord's Prayer. The Rector often condemned the wreckers. Eventually this played on Kate's conscience, and she decided that she would not be party to their evil ways again.

As she sat beside the men in the Goat Inn, on this particular night, she heard the all too familiar words, 'There's a ship in the offing. Here's the lantern. On with your hat and cape.' She hesitated, and a few of the wreckers protested that it was 'no night for a young girl,' but the lantern was placed in her hands and she was ordered to go.

She made her way on to the dangerous rocky causeway and soon she was standing on the cliff-top of Worms Head. She had been taught to walk almost to the end of the cliffs before showing a light and then to come slowly to the edge, moving the lantern up and down. She would continue until a gun fired in Rhosili indicated that her mission was completed. If the tide permitted, she would return across the causeway, but if the narrow causeway was already covered she would have to find shelter and remain on the Head until the tide ebbed.

Suddenly Kate heard the ship below. She thought of the Rector's words and knew she couldn't be party to this evil deed. Nearby was a pile of brushwood, which she kept in case a beacon was needed. Placing the unlit lantern in a cleft in the rocks, she lit the brushwood, and in a few moments the wind fanned a great fire. From the reflected glow, the Captain of the intended victim took his bearings. Soon he was speeding out into the Bristol Channel, on his way to Cardiff.

Kate never returned to Rhosili. A few days later her body was washed ashore, and buried immediately. Some say that she had a nasty gash on her forehead, others say she had fallen into the sea on her return journey, but because she was an orphan, there was no-one to care and so no enquiries were made.

This is where Kate's story should have ended, but many years later an old man dying of a fever in Carmarthen Jail kept calling for Kate. Although he was delirious, he managed to tell the prison chaplain what had happened on that Easter night in 1712. Kate had managed to save the vessel, and the wreckers were furious with her. They raced across the downs and over to the causeway raving and shouting, and one, Bill

Williams, had struck the girl with a boat-hook. The old man was anxious to tell the chaplain that he played no part in her murder. He had merely helped to throw her frail body into the sea.

At Rhosili church one area of the churchyard has no stones in it. It is believed that this was given over to unmarked graves of sailors who had fallen victim to the wreckers.

Another lucrative, although not strictly illegal, trade of the 18th century were the press gangs, who were sent out by the Navy under the command of the junior officer to impress men into the Navy, often with tragic results. Not far from Pwll-ddu (*black-pool*) is an area known as Graves-end, where between seventy and eighty of the press gang victims lost their lives in 1760. They were pressed into serving on *The Caesar*, which left Swansea on the spring tide of 28 November 1760 bound for Plymouth, with Lieutenant James Cobrain in charge. It is believed that they were either bound to the timbers or locked down below under hatches.

No sooner had the ship left Swansea Bay, than the weather began to deteriorate. In the fading light, land was spotted which they assumed to be Mumbles Head. The order was given to pull in and shelter until the weather improved. In fact it was not Mumbles Head, but Pwll-ddu. Once the crew realised their mistake, they tried to turn the ship around, but it was too late. The vessel headed straight for the rocks. It eventually grounded in a spot now known as Caesar's Hole and became a victim of the rising tide. A few survivors managed to scramble ashore to find their way to Pennard, but the villagers knew nothing of the tragedy until the following morning when the remains of the vessel and a number of bodies were washed ashore. Burial of the bodies, between 68-97, was hindered by wreck-pilfering which was commonplace at this time. Eventually the dead were buried in the nearest earth-covered area which is known today as Graves-end, although no memorial exists.

CHAPTER NINE

Communications and The Growth of Gower

Because, being a peninsula, Gower is so remote, the people of Gower did not benefit from integration and mobility that the mainland folk were enjoying. Gower remained isolated until the turn of this century. Even a century ago most Gowerians had never spent a night away from their own cottage and even a journey to Swansea was a major event. A trip to London was an unthinkable experience. C. D. Morgan records in '*Wanderings in Gower*,' that when a farmer from the tip of the peninsula had to go to London on business about 200 years ago, the idea was so awful, that he drew up a will and threw a farewell supper. On his eventual safe return another supper was given and everyone rejoiced. He gained the title of the 'most extraordinary traveller' in Gower and was consulted as a great authority on everything.

At one time, only the Lord of the Manor and the yeoman farmers could afford horses, so the ordinary Gower folk had to be content with a good pair of feet. If they needed to attend to some important business in Swansea, the nearest market town, they would set off from Port Einion walking across the sands, through the valley to Oxwich Green, resting for a while at Oxwich; then along the sands to the stepping stones at Three Cliffs, which would bring them over the dunes to Pennard, through the Mayals and Blackpill, and finally into Swansea.

The roads in Gower were so uneven that wheeled carts were not used until about 1830. Farmers preferred to use packhorses to carry produce to market. Corn was carried in strong bags slung across the animals' backs, whilst the dairy produce was carried in panniers. The girls of the farm would often stand in for their brothers, who were reluctant to make the journey to market, fearing that they would be taken by the press gangs. Many a race took place on the homeward journey with the girls riding side-saddle.

Farmers who could afford the new wheeled carts found that the rough roads were no quicker. Axles and wheels soon broke, which meant expensive repairs as there was little local skill available to mend them. An ordnance survey map of this date shows that there was a network of little roads, many more than we have today, linking every village and farm. Legend has it that once Killay was isolated from Kilvrough, so George Eynon attached his oxen to a wooden plough and ploughed a furrow across Fairwood Common, until he reached the highway from North Gower. This road later became the most favoured route to Swansea from South Gower.

Between 1896 and 1910, people became more mobile when a horse bus service, from Llangennydd to Swansea, was run by the Taylor family. The father and son team first used a converted farm wagon, because they had to deal with crops and livestock as well as passengers. One trip a week was made to Swansea, on a Saturday. Those farmers who could not afford the time would put their produce on the bus and the driver would sell it at Swansea market. In 1910 another member of the family started the first motorbus service between Swansea and Llangennydd, and the last horse-drawn Gower bus made its journey in 1911.

The residents of Port Einion appeared to fare much better for they, according to an advertisement at the end of the last century, had a bus service that ran three times a week.

JOHN GROVE
'BUS PROPRIETOR PORTEYNON

A 'bus leaves Porteynon

on

Monday Morning
Wednesday Morning
Saturday Morning
Returning Every Evening
Special Accommodation

for

Parties of 10 or 50 by Break to any part of Gower
Charges moderate

During the first world war there was a break in operations when buses were commandeered for the war effort. However, the Gower buses still had specially adapted bodies for carrying farm produce, inside and on top.

A unique feature of Gower journeys was the thick white limestone dust, that covered passengers, hedgerows and vehicles alike. People spoke of seeing a large dust-cloud slowly approaching long before they could hear, or see, the approaching bus. Road gangs were regularly employed to fill the roads with limestone and were paid by the weight of limestone broken up, which they did with long-handled hammers. To protect their eyes they wore wire mesh spectacles. At this time not only were the roads rough but the buses were hardly sprung and had solid tyres. Besides being subjected to the white dust, I would imagine you received a good few bruises in the wrong places. It has been said that when two or more vehicles passed in succession, you couldn't see where you were going for about five minutes until the 'white cloud' lifted.

Reports suggest, that 'because of the skill of the roadmen and busmen' a journey from Port Einion to Swansea could be 'as quick as 4 HOURS!' The bus would start at 5 a.m. and arrive in Swansea between 9 and 10 a.m. returning when everyone was ready, which was usually around 4 or 5 in the afternoon. After a long journey home — stopping at every pub *en route* — the bus, packed to the roof with passengers and goods, would reach Port Einion between 10 o'clock and midnight. Besides the passengers and their personal shopping, the load would contain iron bars for the local blacksmith, casks of oil, the odd bag of flour, and even sheets of corrugated iron tied on the roof. People normally only went to Swansea about four times a year, and it was usual to see them standing on the roadside waiting for the bus, to give the driver an order, or to ask him to pass on a message to someone in an adjacent village. I suspect many love-letters to sweethearts were passed in this manner.

The main road, now above the North Gower marsh, was built in the 1920s, where there had been no road before. Around 1922 the Pen-clawdd to Llanmorlais stretch was built, and between then and 1925 it was extended to Llanrhidian to replace the narrow road on the marsh. This marsh route is very attractive even today, although at that time high tides often covered it with water.

After the First World War, the pattern of life changed. People became more time conscious, and this oft-flooded stretch became an inconvenience. Before the war, people were quite content to sit and wait for an hour or so for the water to subside. Impatience made some people try to drive through, with horses plodding sometimes up to their chests in water, and carts half floating. The council placed thick wooden posts to mark where the road was under water, so that carts did not fall into the deep gutters. Some of these post stumps can still be seen today beside the road near Crofty.

Oystermouth entered the history books during the early 19th century when an Act of Parliament was passed on the 28th June 1804 allowing the construction of a railway line from Swansea to Oystermouth, for the 'passage of wagons and other carriages'. It was intended that Mumbles limestone should be carried to Swansea in a wagon pulled by a horse. The Oystermouth Railway and Tramroad Company ran no service over the lines and anyone could use it to haul their own cargo wagons providing they paid a toll. In the spring of 1806, the first horse-drawn goods train travelled from Swansea to Mumbles. Mr Benjamin French, who was involved in the laying of lines, realised the potential of starting a passenger service and offered the Company £20 per year to run a passenger wagon on the line. It was agreed, and it was claimed that on the 25th March 1807, the first passenger railway in the world came into existence.

During its early days an unusual attempt was made to use wind power. The following account appeared in the local newspaper of the day, *The Cambrian*, in 1807:

> "An experiment of a novel kind was made on the Oystermouth Tramroad yesterday, to ascertain the practicability of a carriage proceeding to the Mumbles without horse, by the aid of wind alone. Some Jolly Sons of Neptune rigged a waggon with a long-sail, and the wind blowing strong and as fair as could be wished, set out from our quay, and after clearing the houses dropped anchor at the end of the tramroad in less than three quarters of an hour, having come a distance of about 4½ miles."

The Mumbles Train, as it became known, reached its heyday during the First World War. There were no motor-buses to challenge the service, as these had been taken to aid the war effort, and the use of horses for travelling had long been forgotten. The unique rolling stock gave the railway a charm of its own, as the open-topped tram with 'toast rack' seats trundled along. Passengers would receive a special treat as they passed the Slip and Brynmill where youngsters would turn cart-wheels to the shouts of 'Ha'Penny a Penny O'. The passengers would throw out their half-pennies and pennies and watch the youngsters scramble for the coins. It has been recorded that up to 40,000 people would be carried by the railway on a Bank Holiday.

The line was electrified in April 1929, and the occasion was celebrated by fireworks and dancing on the Mumbles Pier. In the year 1946, a record number of 4,237,000 passengers was carried, but sadly, in 1960 it was all over. Despite objections from the people of Mumbles, the lines were

Mumbles Train arriving at the Mumbles Pier

TO THE GLORY OF GOD
AND IN MEMORY OF
EDGAR EVANS

The plaque erected in memory of Petty Officer Edgar Evans

closed and turned into a seafront footpath. Today there is talk of reviving the old line, certainly adding to the attraction of a thriving leisure industry.

Travel of another kind is remembered in Rhosili Church. On the north wall of the nave there is a memorial to Petty Officer Edgar Evans R.N. who died with Captain Robert Scott on that tragic journey back from the South Pole in 1912. The white marble plaque depicting an Arctic scene was donated by his wife, Lois, nee Beynon, whose father once kept the Old Ship Inn at Middleton. It gives brief details of his death and bears the inscription: 'To see, to strive, to find, and not to yield'.

Captain Scott thought highly of this Gower man, and that is best shown in the words of Scott himself:

> 'Evans, a giant worker with a really remarkable headpiece. It is only now I realise how much has been due to him. Our ski shoes and crampons have been absolutely indispensable, and if the original ideas were not his, the details of manufacture and design and the good workmanship are his alone. He is responsible for every sledge, every sledge fitting, tents, sleeping bags, harness, and when one cannot recall a single expression of dissatisfaction with any one of these items, it shows what an invaluable assistant he has been. Now, besides superintending the putting up of the tent, he thinks out and arranges the packing of the sledge. It is extraordinary how neatly and handily everything is stowed, and how much study has been given to preserving the suppleness and good running qualities of the machine. On the Barrier, before the ponies were killed, he was ever roaming around, correcting faults of storage.'

A fitting accolade, which surely sums up the character of Evans, a true Gowerian.

CHAPTER TEN

Traditional Gower

Gower is steeped in traditional customs, and some were still being practised until the First World War, although not all are unique to the Gower Peninsula.

Yuletide was once a very festive time with many traditions being observed in all corners of Gower. One of the oldest, the Mari Lwyd, meaning *Grey Mare* or *Grey Mary*, was observed a fortnight or so before Christmas. It involved one member of a group of young men wearing a horse's skull, each area having its own skull, fitted with false ears and eyes and decked with ribbons. The eye sockets were fitted with thick bottle glass. The wearer would get beneath a white sheet, and, with the skull fixed above his head, work the jaws, the lower of which had a string and spring fitted to it.

This custom possibly had pagan origins, and continued in places such as Port Einion and Mumbles well into this century. A traditional song was sung, slightly modified in each area, at each farm or cottage. One version is:

> Once I was a young horse,
> And in my stable gay
> I had the best of everything
> Of Barley oats and hay.
> Bur now I am an old horse
> My course is getting small.
> I'm 'bliged to eat the sour grass
> That grows beneath the wall.
>
> Chorus:
> Poor old Horse, let him die
> Poor old Horse, let him die.

> I've eaten all my oats and Hay
> Devoured all my straw,
> I can hardly move about,
> Nor can my carriage draw:
> With these poor weary limbs of mine
> I've travelled many miles
> Over hedges, bramble bushes
> Gates and narrow stiles.
>
> Chorus:
> Poor old Horse, let him die,
> Poor old Horse, let him die.

The men would visit the houses to collect money for charity, although some would pay them not to call. To add to the excitement, the party was refused admittance at first with bolts being firmly drawn across the door. Eventually, a male member of the household would unbolt the door to the screams of the women inside. Once inside the house, the Mari Lwyd would gallop around snapping his jaws, chasing and biting the women. Finally the Mari Lwyd would tire of his fun, normality would resume, and food and drink would be served by the occupants. When it was time to leave, the party would depart singing a verse in Welsh, which when translated went something like this:

> Farewell, gentle folk.
> We have been made welcome,
> God's blessing be upon your house,
> And upon all who dwell therein.

In Mumbles the skull belonging to a horse called Sharper, which had been with the same family for over 100 years, apparently had its original, although slightly yellow, teeth. At Llanmadog after Christmas, the men would bury the skull with mock ceremony in a secret place where it would remain until it was dug up the following year.

A custom unique to Llanmadog was called Holming — 'holmes' being the dialect word for holly. The youngsters would tour the village on 26 December, St Stephen's Day, carrying bunches of holly, and would tickle the legs of any women that they encountered.

On New Year's Eve Gowerians were visited by the Wassailing parties. One of the group would carry a large 'susan' or earthenware pitcher which contained warm spiced ale, the container wrapped in a sheepskin or blanket to retain its heat. At the door of the homestead a Wassail song was

The Mari Lwyd

sung, which asked for a blessing on the farmer, his crops and stock for the coming year. The party was welcomed and invited in. The wassailers would decant some of the ale into a wassail bowl, sharing the ale with the residents. Before leaving the house, the pitcher was topped up with more hot spiced ale in readiness for the next house. Gifts of money were given to the wassailers, who would leave thanking the household for their hospitality in song.

Another very old custom was the Mabsant or Saint Day which was a traditional North Gower event. Mabsant, Welsh for Patron Saint, is a remnant of Celtic times. Its origin was probably pagan before being taken over and modified by the Christian church. By the 19th century, however, the religious meaning had vanished completely and Mabsants were just an excuse for a rowdy village get-together.

The various villages celebrated their Mabsants on their local Saint's Day. Llangennydd on 5 July — St Cennydd's day, Rhosili on 12 February, and Llanmadog on the 12 November. It is recorded that the Rev J. D. Davies enjoyed and joined in these festivities, whereas one of his contempories, William Griffiths the Methodist minister, said in 1819 that 'It was an ungodly gathering and a meeting of the devil for drinking and dancing.'

The occasion would be started by lighting the bonfire on the evening before the Mabsant day. Dancing, ball games, cock fighting and prize fighting were the highlights, and the evening would be rounded off with a Gower reel. The celebrations would last three days, with people coming from all over Gower and even from Swansea to join in. Each village had a traditional dish. At Llangennydd it was 'whitepot', a mixture of flour, milk and currants blended together and baked in a brick oven, said to commemorate the milk that flowed from St Cennydd's Titty Bell. Rhosili's speciality was a kind of plum pudding called a 'bonny clobby', and Llanmadog's was a pie made from chopped mutton and currants.

At Llangennydd, a pole would be attached to the church tower and a wooden cock, covered in white calico with scarlet and blue ribbons, raised. This purported to represent the birds that looked after St Cennydd on his journey to Worm's Head. The Mabsant continued into the 19th century but, towards the end, the decorated cock was set up outside the churchyard because the celebrations became too noisy for the minister. In 1888 the tower was repaired, and the holes where the wooden cock was hoisted were carefully preserved and still visible today.

A novel way of inviting people to a Gower wedding was by song. This was called a Bidding Wedding and a 'Bidder' would sing a formal invitation at the homes of those invited.

As soon as the wedding was announced, brewing would commence at the Wedding House, a building such as a barn, chosen for its size. Until the wedding the brew was sold, and the proceeds given to the young brides. (Both bride and groom were known as brides.)

On the eve of the wedding relatives would visit and bring gifts of currant loaves. These were cut into slices and sold at the wedding supper to the young men who would present them to maidens of their choice. Later that evening, the girls would display their collection of currant slices and the one with the largest number of slices would be declared the 'Belle of the Ball.'

After the wedding ceremony the guests and brides proceeded to the Wedding House. On the way the procession would be imprisoned by a rope or chain held across the path until they scattered a handful of coins. There is a similar tradition in Dunster, an ancient Norman town in Somerset, so maybe it originated with the Normans.

At the Wedding House, gifts were made to the 'Brides'. Money would be given or heaved, which means to donate on the understanding that the couple would repay it when the donor or someone in the donor's family got married. The sum donated would be called out and officially received by the Bidder, who would enter it into a ledger. As much as £100 would be collected, sufficient in those days to set the couple up in married life. Many people gave generously, using this as an insurance policy against their own wedding. After the bidding there would be the usual wedding feast and dancing. The last Bidding Wedding was held at Llanddewi in 1906, and one of the last 'Bidders' was Phil Tanner. He was well known in Gower and carried a staff decorated with red, white and blue ribbons as he visited each invited home chanting the invitation. Only a short time before his death in 1950, at the age of 88, he recorded some of his songs for posterity. A traditional bidding song would go as follows:

I'm a messenger to you and the whole house in general,
To invite you to the wedding of Morgan Eynon and Nancy Hopkins,
The wedding which will be next Thursday fortnight,
The wedding house will be the Ship Inn Port Einion
Where the Brides will take breakfast on plenty of good bread, butter and cheese,
Walk to Port Einion Church to get married, back and take dinner,

And then I'll see if I can get you some good tin meat and some good attendance

And whatever you wish to give at the dinner-table the brides will be thankful for.

There will be a fiddle in attendance, for there'll be plenty of Music there, and dancing if you'll come and dance.

There'll be fiddlers, fifers, drummers and the devil don't know what besides

I don't know what.

There'll be plenty of drinkables there, so they
tell me, but that
I haven't tasted.

And if you'll come to the wedding
I'll do all that lie in my power that evening if
required

To get you a sweetheart apiece, if I don't get
drunk,

But the brides is wishful you should come or send.

The 'tin-meat' mentioned in the song is not tinned meat as we know it today, but a traditional dish of mutton. Mutton would be placed in a large shallow tin, covered with a layer of pastry, and baked in a brick oven. Those guests who attended the wedding supper would buy their 'tin-meat' at the table, one tin costing five shillings and being sufficient for four. No one in the village was forgotten, and portions of the 'tin-meat' would be distributed to anyone unable to attend.

Another well known tradition concerns the legendary Gower Fairies or Verry Folks. At Broughton Bay is Lagadranta Farm, from the Welsh meaning 'eye of the stream', reputed to be the last place visited by the fairies. The story goes that an old woman called at the farm and asked the farmer's wife for the loan of a sieve, but she didn't have one. The woman told her 'I'll take the one you have there over the vat straining hops.' Suspecting that the old woman was one of the Gower Verry Folk, because it was a well known fact that they used sieves 'for to sifty gold', and knowing that it was extremely unlucky not to help the fairies, the woman immediately handed over the sieve. A few days later the old woman returned the sieve and told the farmer's wife that 'Since you were so good as to lend it to me, the biggest cask in your house shall never be without beer'. Telling the farmer's wife not to let anyone know the secret, she

Kennixton Farmhouse, a typical Gower farmhouse

Inside a typical Gower farmhouse

walked towards the well and disappeared into the deep below. For weeks, Lagadranta Farm revelled in free beer until the farmer's wife could not resist bragging to her neighbour. Immediately the supply of beer dried up. She was not very popular with the men of the village.

Another fable tells of the tenant of Eynon's Ford Farm who woke one night hearing music. Looking out of the window he saw that his cowshed was teeming with little folk, the Verry Folk, dressed in scarlet and green. The farmer was so surprised that he stood there watching as they danced around a fat ox. Suddenly he realised they were preparing to kill the animal. Horrified he tried to move, but he found himself riveted to the spot. The Verry Folk expertly killed the ox and dressed the animal ready for eating. After the great feast, he watched as they collected the bones and hide. They carefully checked the bones, and found that one small leg bone was missing. They searched frantically, tearing at their hair and throwing their arms about wildly. Exhausted they gave up, placed the bones in the skeleton position, and finally stretched the hide over them. To the farmer's amazement, the ox fattened and came alive. Soon after, he fell asleep. Later, when leading the ox out to pasture, he noticed that the animal had a slight lameness. He remembered his 'dream' and the missing small bone.

Souling Day was celebrated on 12 November and on the 1 November most Gower wives would begin baking Souly cakes in readiness for the day. On the evening of the 12th, youngsters of the village would visit their neighbours and sing:

> Souly Souly, Christendom
> Every good lady give me some
> Give me some or give me none
> Give me an answer and I'll be gone
> If you haven't got a penny
> a ha'penny will do.
> If you haven't got a ha'penny
> God bless you.

The 'Soulers' reward would be a souly cake or money. The origin of this custom is unknown, but it is possible that before the calendar was changed in the mid 18th century, the 12 November would have been the 1 November, All Soul's Day.

Until the 1880's, the 1 September was a day of celebration in Oystermouth when the Bread and Cheese Fair was held. By tradition the skiff owners would treat their crews to bread, cheese and beer, and there would be a variety of events to entertain. These would include punt races, diving, swimming and greasy pole competitions. The children were not forgotten either, but their competition to build a 'grotto' would last throughout the season. The grotto would be made from oyster shells, collected from visitors buying oysters from the stalls along the seafront, decorated with seaweed and lit from inside with a candle.

Today, the Gower Agricultural Society brings Gower alive at the Annual Gower Show held at Penrice Castle. In 1664, Charles II granted a charter to Sir Edward Mansel of Oxwich allowing him to hold two weekly markets and four fairs annually at Penrice, although it is not certain if Sir Edward did hold all four fairs. In September, the grounds of Penrice are teeming with the finest cattle, sheep and pigs that the peninsula can muster. Sheep-dogs exhibit their masterly control over the sheep, while inside the marquees homemade jams, honey and fresh vegetables compete for the attention of the purchasing public.

There is no end to the story of Gower. Although it has encountered invaders, storms and shipwrecking, and is steeped in history and traditions, it still remains unspoilt and unhurried, retaining its place in today's modern society.

Now you've read the book, discover Gower for yourself. You won't be disappointed.

Selected Bibliography

Lloyd, J. E., *A History of Wales* (Ernest Benn 1930)
Phillips, Olive, *Gower* (Robert Hale 1956)
Morton, E. V., *(In Search of Wales)* (Methuen 1932)
Walker, David, *Medieval Wales* (Cambridge University Press 1990)
Morgan, C. D., *Wandering in Gower* (1886)
Tucker, H. M., *Gower Gleaning* (The Gower Society 1951)
Journals of the Gower Society
Leland, John, *Itinerary* (1536-39)
Lucas, R. L. T., *A Gower Family* (The Book Guild 1986)
The Normans in Glamorgan, Gower and Kidweli 1936

Acknowledgements

All illustrations copyright of C. Hughes, except:

Paviland Cave, Farming Settlement, Bronze Age hut, Ring brooch
(National Museum of Wales)

Cockle Women, Mumbles Train, Mari Lwyd,
Kennixton Farmhouse and interior
(Welsh Folk Museum)

Cover photograph:
(by Joan Gravell on behalf of the National Trust)